JOHN CHRYSOSTOM

--ON VIRGINITY

--AGAINST REMARRIAGE

Translation by Sally Rieger Shore

with an Introduction by Elizabeth A. Clark

Studies in Women and Religion
Volume Nine

The Edwin Mellen Press
New York and Toronto

Library of Congress Cataloging in Publication Data

John Chrysostom, Saint, d. 407
    On virginity ; Against remarriage.

    (Studies in women and religion ; v. 9)
    Translation of: On virginity and Against remarriage.
    Includes bibliographical references.
    1. Virginity--Religious aspects--Christianity.
2. Celibacy. 3. Remarriage--religious aspects--
Christianity. I. Clark, Elizabeth A. (Elizabeth Ann),
1938-   . II. Shore, Sally Rieger. III. John
Chrysostom, Saint, d. 407. Peri monandrias. English.
1983. IV. Title. V. Series.
BR65.C45D43 1983   248.4'7   83-8193
ISBN 0-88946-543-6

Studies in Women and Religion   ISBN 0-88946-549-5

The Edwin Mellen Press
P.O. Box 450
Lewiston, New York 14092

Printed in the United States of America

ACKNOWLEDGMENTS

The translator and the introducer of this volume would like to acknowledge several persons whose assistance was important in its preparation. Sally Rieger Shore wishes to thank her dissertation advisor, Father Thomas Halton of the Department of Greek and Latin, The Catholic University of America, for his guidance. A debt of gratitude is also owed to two of her former professors, the late Doris Bishop and the late Bernard Peebles, for their inspiration. Mary Ann Ellery deserves a word of recognition as well for the help she provided regarding facilities at the Library of Congress. Elizabeth Clark would like to add her thanks to the staffs of the Dumbarton Oaks and the Union Theological Seminary (New York) libraries for their help. Sally Rieger Shore and Elizabeth Clark both thank Mrs. Una Crist for her efficient typing of the manuscript.

A fuller discussion of John Chrysostom's views on women and sexuality than is contained in the following introduction can be found in Elizabeth Clark's *Jerome, Chrysostom, and Friends: Essays and Translations* (The Edwin Mellen Press, 1979).

CONTENTS

INTRODUCTION

Elizabeth A. Clark

John Chrysostom—so called for his "golden-mouthed" oratory[1]—composed more treatises on asceticism and marriage than any other Greek-writing church father. Because of his enormous literary production and his eventful life, we are better acquainted with Chrysostom than we are with many other ancient figures. Although the sources leave some basic questions unanswered, and the highly rhetorical style in which Chrysostom wrote, heady with exaggeration, numbs the modern reader, our knowledge of his life and ascetic concerns is nonetheless pertinent to understanding his treatises *On Virginity* and *Against Remarriage*, here published in English translation for the first time.

Chrysostom's contemporaries or near-contemporaries Palladius, Socrates, Sozomen, and Theodoret commented on his life, yet their notices leave modern scholars uncertain as to the date of his birth: estimates have ranged from A.D. 344 to 354.[2] Although the traditional reading of these ancient histories took Chrysostom's father, Socundus, to be *magister militum* of Syria,[3] A. H. M. Jones has more recently argued that Secundus should be demoted to a "high grade civil servant."[4] If Jones' interpretation is correct, the reports of Socrates and Sozomen that Chrysostom came from a noble family may need reassessment.[5] In any event, Secundus died a few years after his marriage, leaving his twenty-year-old widow, Anthusa, with

two small children.[6] The patristic sources add that
Chrysostom trained for the bar[7] or (in an alternate interpretation) for work in the office of an imperial clerk.[8]
Some also state that he studied with the famous rhetorician
of Antioch, Libanius,[9] and with the philosopher Andragathius.[1]

Antioch, the city of Chrysostom's birth and upbringing, was a thriving Syriac metropolis of perhaps 200,000
persons. Until Constantinople's rise in the fourth century, it had been the third city of the Empire, ranking
behind only Rome and Alexandria.[11] Christians, Jews, and
pagans all flourished there.[12] By decree of the Council
of Nicaea in A.D. 325, it had been made a patriarchate
whose territory was co-extensive with the civil diocese
of the Orient.[13] Chrysostom's baptism when he was about
eighteen years old[14] and his subsequent training by Christian teachers, including the noted Biblical scholar,
Diodore of Tarsus,[15] took place in Antioch.

From his youth, Chrysostom showed a keen personal
interest in asceticism.[16] Palladius notes that John
spent four of his formative years under the tutelage of
an ascetic named Syrus in monastic retreat on the moun-
tains outside Antioch. For another two years, Chrysostom
lived a solitary's life in a cave.[17] Only ill-health,
brought on by his rigorous regimen, convinced him to
abandon eremiticism and return to Antioch.[18] Probably
already a lector in the church at Antioch before his retreat to the wilderness,[19] Chrysostom upon his return was
ordained deacon in A.D. 381 and, five years later,
priest.[20] It was in his Antiochene period, most likely
when he served as deacon, that Chrysostom composed his
first treatises advocating asceticism, including the two
contained in this volume.[21]

The better-known and more eventful portion of Chrysostom's life falls after his call to the bishopric of

Constantinople in A.D. 397. His struggles there with
other clergy, royalty, and the unregenerate rich, the attack upon him by Theophilus of Alexandria, and his two
sentences of exile (the last of which also saw his death
in A.D. 407) are more fully covered by the ancient historians than his earlier years.[22] It is nonetheless
clear that he manifested a strong ascetic bent from the
time of his baptism to that of his downfall—indeed, according to Palladius, his downfall was in part occasioned
by the ascetic reforms he pressed upon his reluctant
clergy and the "society Christians" of Constantinople.[23]
Commentators agree that during his years as cleric at
Antioch, Chrysostom was exceptionally keen for the ascetic life.[24] Later, as priest and bishop, he toned down
his advocacy of rigorous asceticism[25] and adopted a view
that has been described as less "eschatological" and more
"incarnational."[26]

In addition to the treatises that comprise this volume, Chrysostom wrote other works during his years at
Antioch that manifest similar ascetic themes. In the *Comparison of the Power, Riches, and Excellence of a King and
a Monk,* for example, Chrysostom, adapting motifs from
Stoic diatribe, argues that a monk who practices the
"philosophic" virtues of Christianity, defined in accordance with asceticism, is truly more regal than the monarch
engaged in the cares of the world.[27] Whereas the king
fights mere barbarians, the monk casts down demons;[28] the
king's possessions are buried with this life, while the
monk's spiritual wealth lasts eternally,[29] and so forth.
In *Against the Opponents of the Monastic Life,* Chrysostom
wars against those who succumb to the love of riches and to
sexual desire[30] (pederasty receives special condemnation).[31]
Similarly, he advocated in his *Letter to a Young Widow,*
composed in A.D. 380 or 381, that widows not remarry.[32]

Two early letters Chrysostom wrote to a "fallen" friend,
Theodore, also counsel sexual denial: Theodore, having
lapsed from his ascetic commitment through his passion
for a certain Hermione, is urged by Chrysostom to abandon
her and return to the ascetic life.[33] In addition, at
least one of Chrysostom's two treatises against "spiritual marriage" (the practice of ascetic men and women
living together) may have been composed during the 380s
in Antioch.[34] Later in Chrysostom's career, his numerous
commentaries and homilies on Genesis and the New Testament books, as well as his homilies praising female
saints and martyrs, all resound with ascetic themes. Thus
On Virginity (dated to the 380s or the early 390s)[35] and
Against Remarriage (dated A.D. 383-386)[36] are in the
company of many other writings by Chrysostom that cele-
brate the ascetic life. To be sure, his championing of
virginity was far from novel in his time. In fact,
scholars think his treatise *On Virginity* borrowed themes
from similar works composed a few years earlier by Basil
of Ancyra,[37] Eusebius of Emesa,[38] and Gregory of Nyssa.[39]
Chrysostom's treatises translated below, then, are just
one manifestation of the ascetic fervor of late ancient
Christianity.

Enough manuscripts remain of the two treatises here
translated (some of which date to the tenth century)[40]
to ensure reasonable confidence in the Greek text. The
Greek texts used by Sally Shore for her translation are
those established by Herbert Musurillo for *On Virginity* and by Gerard Ettlinger for *Against Remarriage*
and published in volumes 125 and 138, respectively,
of Sources Chrétiennes.[41]

II

Although it has been posited that Chrysostom's

treatise *On Virginity* can be read as an extended
commentary on I Corinthians 7,[42] it is immediately
apparent to the contemporary reader that it consti-
tutes no simple explication of the Pauline text, no more
than *Against Remarriage* does.   Despite Chrysostom's constant appeal to Paul, so changed was the intellectual and
social setting of late fourth-century Christianity that
his interpretation of I Corinthians would no doubt have
startled its author in several ways.   It is not simply
the passage of time that separates Chrysostom from Paul.
Chrysostom's fine training in Greek literature and philosophy[43] was far superior to whatever rudimentary classical
education we may imagine Paul received.   In addition, his
position as deacon and priest in the church of Antioch
involved him in an ecclesiastical organization much
larger and more elaborately structured than that of Corinth in the mid-first century.   Yet these and other fac-
tors mean little in themselves unless we appreciate what
such changes signalled for Chrysostom's understanding of
Paul.

In I Corinthians 7, Paul made clear that despite
the usefulness of marriage as a check for sexual desire,
celibacy was preferable.[44]   He hoped that Christians
would choose his path of celibacy as the one most expedi-
tious for the period before the eschaton's arrival.[45]   By
the late fourth century, celibacy was considered the most
exalted way of life for Christians.   Virginity and widowhood were no longer, as Paul saw them, simply conditions
in which persons might best preserve their energies for
the service of the Lord; they were now "professions" for
which a solemn pledge was taken.   Chrysostom thus has
something more definite in mind when he speaks of widows
and virgins than Paul apparently did.   For example, when
commenting on Paul's opinion that a virgin did not sin if

she married,[46] Chrysostom feels constrained to remark that
Paul most certainly could not have been speaking of a girl
who had formally renounced marriage for virginity, for if
such a girl were to wed, she would be committing an unforgivable sin. Rather, on Chrysostom's reading of the passage, Paul intended to characterize a young woman who had
not yet decided whether to marry or to profess virginity.[47]
Likewise for widows: Paul could not mean (according to
Chrysostom) that a woman who had vowed herself to perpetual widowhood in the Christian church was still free to
remarry.[48] To pledge oneself in widowhood while contem-
plating a second marriage would be to break a promise.[49]
It is evident that to be a virgin or a widow in Chrysostom's time implied a more fixed status than it had in
Paul's.

Although when Chrysostom wrote the treatises under
consideration there were only a few monasteries for women
in Asia Minor,[50] many women committed to a celibate life
had banded together in groups or had simply continued to
live in their families' homes.[51] We know less than we
wish about early monasticism for women in the area. Yet
churches supported massive numbers of such female celibates, as is revealed by Chrysostom's chance comment that
3000 widows and virgins were assisted by the church at
Antioch.[52] The ascetic fervor that attended the cessation of the persecutions and the sudden acceptance of the
Christian faith is a familiar theme to historians of late
antiquity; whatever reasons may be posited for the phenom-
enon, it is clearly attested in the sources. Whether or
not *On Virginity* was written for the explicit purpose of
recruiting virgins,[53] it nonetheless depicts the rewards
of celibacy and the difficulties of marriage in ways that
must have been attractive to many Christians of Chrysostom's age.

Although Chrysostom agreed with Paul that celibacy
was preferable to marriage, their reasons differed:
Paul's view that virginity should be favored because of
the imminence of the eschaton was re-interpreted by
Chrysostom to fit a late fourth-century context. Paul
believed, as he set forth in I Thessalonians 4:15, that
Jesus would return to usher in the Kingdom of God during
the lifetimes of many in his audience. Thus it is not
surprising to find him in I Corinthians 7 arguing that
because of the "impending distress" the single state was
to be advocated. Since the time had "grown short," as
Paul put it, it would be better not to entangle oneself
in marriage, for the unmarried person was freer to
serve the Lord in the brief interim before the Kingdom's
arrival.[54]

Chrysostom's treatment of Paul's words reminds us
how rapidly the eschatological hope of early Christianity
faded, how speedily the enthusiasts for the Kingdom's arrival were viewed as unpopular eccentrics, if not worse.[55]
So removed from Paul's eschatological expectation is
Chrysostom that he cannot comprehend the plain meaning of
the text. Since he, like his contemporaries, no longer
expected an immediate cessation of this world, all Paul's
comments about the eschaton must be understood as per-
taining to the individual's afterlife in heaven. Indeed,
Chrysostom addresses the (to him) puzzling problem of
why Paul only seemed to speak of celibacy's advantages
for the present life, rather than of those for the next.[56]
Chrysostom's answer is that Paul's approach was conditioned by pedagogical considerations: since people tend
to be more concerned with the here-and-now than with the
heavenly afterlife, Paul, skillful teacher that he was,
leads them from their present lowly concerns to a higher
"philosophy" (Chrysostom's customary term for Christian

truth) by addressing their immediate anxieties first.[57]
Chrysostom is quick to admit that virginity has its present advantages, as Paul had suggested,[58] but the future
rewards in heaven capture his imagination at least
equally.[59] The account we must give of ourselves in the
heavenly court, before the divine Judge, he thinks,
should always weigh on our minds—and that judgment will
take place upon an individual's death, not at the eschaton's arrival.[60]

This change in eschatological expectation forms the
background to two prominent themes reiterated throughout
Chrysostom's works: that while we live on this earth, we
are to lead the life of the angels as much as possible
if we wish to join them in their heavenly home later,[61]
and that celibate women can expect to greet Jesus as
their Bridegroom when they enter the heavenly mansions
after death.[62] The motivation for celibacy, in other
words, has been significantly altered since the time of
Paul. No longer seen primarily as a practical measure to
expedite Christian living while we await God's Kingdom,
celibacy has now acquired an "ontological" status that
raises humans to a semi-divine existence in the midst of
the present era and prepares them for incorporation into
the ranks of those angelic powers who Jesus allegedly
declared neither married nor gave in marriage.[63]

If virginity or celibacy was viewed as an "angelic"
way of life, it is easy to understand why Chrysostom
thought it more elevated than marriage. Yet in a neat
inversion of his own argument, he posits that virginity
is the true *human* condition, not just the angelic one.
Virginity was the condition in which Adam and Eve were
created and in which God had intended that they remain.[64]
By adopting virginity, we not only become more godly, we
are also recalled to our true human nature. Chrysostom

elaborates this point at some length. Sexual desire, he
says, was not "naturally" implanted in humans at their
creation as part of their biological constitution.[65]   It,
along with marriage and sexual reproduction, resulted
from the Fall in the Garden of Eden[66]—a view that Paul
would no doubt have found astounding. Although Paul had
suggested in Romans 5 that death entered the world
through the sin of Adam, he nowhere hinted at Chrysostom's conclusion, that marriage was introduced only as a
consequence of the Fall. Yet Chrysostom, using Hesiod's
image of Decency and Reverence abandoning the earth at
the end of the Golden Age,[67] described the Fall as the
time when the beauty of virginity abandoned the first
couple, leaving them to become "earth and ashes"—and to
discover the solace of marriage.[68] As Chrysostom bluntly
put it, "For where death is, there is marriage."[69]   To
the obvious question of how the human race could have
multiplied without sexual intercourse, Chrysostom an-
swered that God could have created other humans without
recourse to sexual means, just as he created the angels
and archangels (who suffer no population deficiency),
and, for that matter, as he created Adam and Eve.[70] Fur-
thermore, Christians should understand that children are
never simply begotten by "natural" means in marriage;
their creation is always by God's will and word, as is
made clear by such Old Testament examples as Abraham and
Sarah's belated conception of Isaac.[71] In any case, the
Bible teaches us that it is not the lack of sexual intercourse that brings about the demise of the human race,
but rather sin, as we can see in the case of Noah's
flood.[72]

Since the Fall, the two functions that marriage
serves are procreation and the taming of sexual desire.[73]
For Chrysostom, both are dubious justifications for the

marital state. He notes that for Christians who look to
a heavenly afterlife, the desire for children is an in-
appropriate motivation for marriage.[74] Chrysostom notes
that Paul himself never mentioned the production of children as a justification for marriage: the only rationale
the apostle gave for marriage was the containment of sexual desire[75]—or, as Chrysostom more crudely puts it, for
"the suppression of licentiousness and debauchery."[76]
Marriage, a concession to our weakness,[77] a rescue from
impurity,[78] is for those who are still "caught up in
their passions, who desire to live the life of swine and
be ruined in brothels."[79]

Yet Chrysostom's view of marriage is not wholly
negative. Marriage was useful in its time, he concedes.
In the "childhood" of our race, we needed such infant fare.
But, like fledglings, we must learn to fly and leave the
maternal nest.[80] Chrysostom here bases his argument on
Paul's: that Christians must become adults and put away
"childish things,"[81] yet they must be given "milk" before
they are ready for "solid food."[82] Marriage, then, for
Chrysostom, was one of the indulgences allowed by the Old
Law, i.e., the Old Testament.[83] It does not detract from
the relative goodness of marriage that now a more perfect
standard is recommended to us, one consonant with the
greater overflow of the Spirit's power since the advent
of Christ.[84]

Chrysostom's eagerness to defend marriage as a relative good despite its disadvantages stems in large part
from the battle the orthodox church had waged in earlier
years against the Gnostics' depreciation of the created
world; in Chrysostom's time, the struggle persisted
against the Manichean ascetics.[85] Although Paul in I
Corinthians may have addressed an ascetic contingent who
disapproved of marriage,[86] it is unlikely that he was

confronting a full-blown Gnostic attack on marriage.
Later New Testament writings hint that the attack on marriage may have become more acute after Paul's time.[87]
Certainly the church fathers from the late second century
on had to take care that their negative remarks about
marriage not be interpreted as supporting the views attributed to some Gnostics that human sexual functioning,
reproduction, and marriage were traps set by the evil
powers to ensnare humans.[88] In *On Virginity,* Chrysostom
singles out Marcion, Valentinus, and Mani as the three
heretical leaders who, he says, led their followers to
eternal perdition through their teaching about the created order, virginity, and marriage.[89] The burden of
Chrysostom's complaint is that the ascetic heretics are
wrongly motivated in their espousal of virginity:[90] they
insult God[91] and slander his creation by treating marriage with such contempt.[92] The heretics, he argues, are
almost compelled to lives of virginity because of their
desire to abstain from the evil of marriage,[93] whereas
true virtue must be more than simple abstention from
evil.[94] In fact, the heretics inadvertently reduce the
glory of virginity by their deprecation of marriage, for
if virginity is understood merely as better than something inferior, i.e., marriage, it cannot be viewed as a
very laudable end.[95] Chrysostom's argument that praising
marriage also serves to glorify virginity[96] should be
understood in the context of his anti-Gnostic polemic.
Indeed, it was imperative for Chrysostom to uphold the
goodness of marriage, amid his many criticisms of it, if
he himself wished to avoid charges of Manicheanism.[97]
Thus the conflict of orthodox Christianity with Gnostic
and Manichean groups after the time of Paul added a di-
mension to the debate on marriage that was absent from
the apostle's arguments.

Still another way in which Chrysostom's discussion of marriage and celibacy differs from Paul's lies in Chrysostom's attitudes toward women. Paul's views on the female sex have been much debated in recent years,[98] but even taking Paul at his most conservative, we find nothing in the genuinely Pauline epistles to rival the deprecating comments Chrysostom makes about Eve and her descendants. For example, Paul in Romans writes of Adam's sin and its consequences for the human race, but does not mention Eve in this passage.[99] Chrysostom, however, attributing the derogatory comments about women in the Pastoral Epistles to Paul,[100] blames Eve for her treachery in the sin.[101] It was she who subjected man to death.[102] It was women who were the cause of the Great Flood and who destroyed, or attempted to destroy, the Old Testament heroes.[103] Woman at creation was intended to be a helper to man,[104] but she did not adhere to this high purpose.[105] She now "helps" man by bearing his children and allaying his sexual desire, but Chrysostom scoffs at the worth of such assistance to Christians.[106] Women who still make "the demands of wives" rather than embracing chaste frugality are in fact dangers to their husbands, not aids.[107] To be sure, Chrysostom's words about women are not entirely condemnatory; he can even sympathize with the oppression and outright cruelty to which they are often subjected in marriage.[108] Nonetheless, his views on Eve and other women are far more biting than anything in Paul's letters.

Lastly, Chrysostom's views on marriage and virginity are influenced by some features of late ancient ethical discussion that had made little if any impact on Paul's thinking. To begin, we should note that Chrysostom thinks of Christian teaching not so much as divine revelation as "philosophy,"[109] indeed, as the highest

imaginable wisdom. As such, Christianity had both its
theoria and its *praxis:* it taught the loftiest contemplation, yet offered sage advice for daily living. To cast
the discussion of virginity and marriage in the framework
of "philosophy" gives it a decidedly abstract flavor that
was foreign to Paul's advice, geared to address a pressing
practical problem. Chrysostom's discussion throughout
shows that he borrows from the traditions of Greek philosophy. For example, he adapts Plato's image in *Phaedrus*
246A-248E of reason as the charioteer reining in the unruly
horses of the passions to describe the virgin who as charioteer keeps the "horses" of her tongue, her ears, her feet,
and so forth, under control.[110] An appeal to revelation
has here been supplanted by an appeal to Greek ethical
writings. Likewise, Chrysostom's treatment of riches is in
strict accord with the classical praises of simple living
(whose benefits include good health, hearty appetite, sound
sleep)[111] that are more reminiscent of Stoic and Cynic
diatribe[112] than of the New Testament.

  Nowhere is the influence of the Greek ethical tradition more prominent in Chrysostom's writings than in his
discussion of the relationship between virtue and free
choice. Behind Chrysostom's insistence that virtue is not
genuine if it is not freely chosen, the result of reasoned
decision, lies the entire Greek ethical tradition from Socrates onward.[113] Only when we make a decision can we be
credited with acting well, Chrysostom argues.[114] So strong
was Chrysostom's desire to emphasize the role of choice[115]
that modern commentators have sometimes felt obliged to defend him from charges of Semi-Pelagianism.[116] Indeed, when
we note how sharply Chrysostom must bend Paul's words to
make the apostle's celibacy a matter of his own choice and
effort, not (as Paul himself said) a gift from God, we can
see the point of the charge. Chrysostom thus argues that

when Paul attributed his virginity to God's gift, he was
simply exhibiting humility. What Paul calls "gifts" are
really virtuous deeds. Paul's continence resulted from
his own effort. Chrysostom remarks that he stresses this
point so that no one will imagine that he or she need not
strive in order to uphold celibacy.[117] Paul thus functions as a model for others who struggle to live without
sexual relation.[118]

Chrysostom's emphasis on personal effort is important for his advocacy of virginity and widowhood: they
are states of life that are (in the Stoic phrase he borrowed) "up to us."[119] If we do not exercise sexual self-
control, we have only ourselves to blame and must concede
that we simply did not make the effort,[120] an effort that
must not be postponed if we are to receive the appropriate heavenly crown.[121] The decision for celibacy must be
a completely free one.[122] No one should imagine, for example, that a widow could be "compelled" to remarry.[123]
There is no "compulsion" involved in her choice. And if
she makes the decision for celibacy, there can be no going back on it without her breaking a solemn promise to
God.[124] Chrysostom compares the choice of celibacy to an
athlete's decision to enter a contest: the athlete freely
decides whether or not to participate, but once he enters
the stadium, there is no more choice; the "law of the
contest" then prevails.[125]

Chrysostom's insistence that celibacy must involve
free decision accords well with his understanding of virginity and widowhood as governed by the "counsels of perfection."[126] In the patristic era, the notion became common that not all of the ethical injunctions given in the
New Testament need be taken in their strictest sense by
every Christian. There was a minimum standard of morality incumbent upon all Christians, to be sure: no Chris-

tian should murder, steal, deny the faith, and so forth.
But it was understood that only some Christians would be
strong enough to renounce property and the sexual life.
For those willing to accept and act upon those "counsels
of perfection," a more glorious reward in heaven was en-
visaged. This double-tiered concept of merit was particularly prominent in the church fathers' discussions of
marriage and virginity. For Chrysostom, Christians are
of course permitted to marry, although marriage should
never be viewed as an opportunity for sexual excess or
soft living.[127] But those who opt for the more perfect
way can expect a more brilliant reception in heaven.[128]
And if graded rewards are available to Christians, it is
important that celibacy with its highest reward be a
freely-chosen state. As Chrysostom phrased it, Christ
quite intentionally did not compel people to virginity by
making it a law for all his followers, since then no
"honor" would have been attached to the state: virginity
would simply have been a duty required of all Christians.[129]

In *On Virginity*, Chrysostom uses the argument link-
ing celibacy and free choice to good effect in his opening attack against the heretical virgins: they are not
really virgins since they have not chosen their virginal
condition.[130] Because they view marriage as an evil,
they have not made a genuine decision for virginity. Yet
by their avoidance of the perceived evil of marriage,
they have deprived themselves of the reward they expected
to receive since they did not freely choose the virginal
life.[131] Such heretics want to make virginity an obligation, not a matter of virtuous choice, and herein lies
the error of their position.[132] Chrysostom points out
that Paul, unlike the heretics, never spoke of marital
intercourse as defiling; according to Chrysostom, Paul

rather believed that sex was simply a waste of one's
time.[133] If marriage is not a genuinely good option for
Christians, Chrysostom continues, it makes no sense to
praise virgins, no more than we laud eunuchs for their
sexual chastity. Indeed, heretical virgins share mutilation with eunuchs, for although the latter have suffered
bodily castration, the heretical virgins have had their
"upright thoughts" cut off by the devil![134]

   The moral framework within which Chrysostom con-
structs his argument about virtue's link with choice is
thus significantly different from that of Paul, whose
ethical position rested on a belief that God gave various
spiritual gifts (*charismata*) to different Christians for
the upbuilding of the community.[135] To some, like Paul,
the Spirit had granted a gift of celibacy, but not all
would receive that gift and hence not all could be expected to follow his course.[136] Although Chrysostom in
his voluminous writings speaks much of grace, on the issue of celibacy he emphasizes human effort almost exclusively. He stresses the "up-to-us"-ness of human action
as much as the Stoic philosophers did, for he, like they,
believed that praise and blame could not be assigned unless virtuous action were freely chosen or rejected.[137]

   A third aspect of Chrysostom's writings on celibacy
that is directly borrowed from the world of classical
literature—an aspect that does not appear in Paul's letters—are the *topoi* on marriage, the common-place examples and arguments that highlighted the problems occasioned by marriage and wives. Although Paul, for his
part, thinks of marriage as a bond between the partners,[138]
and mentions the worldly anxieties that marriage may
bring,[139] he does not belabor the disadvantages—indeed,
the horrors—of the married estate as Chrysostom, following many classical writers, does. Especially in

describing the woes of marriage Chrysostom makes free use
of the commonplaces to be found in classical literature.[140] In doing so, Chrysostom goes far beyond Paul's
modestly expressed view that marriage was a "bond." Thus
according to Chrysostom, marriage is even worse than
slavery: slaves have the hope that they can buy their
freedom, but for the married there is no such escape, since
divorce is not permitted to Christians.[141] In an out-
burst of rhetorical extravagance, Chrysostom compares
married couples to fugitive slaves whose legs have been
shackled together: if they wish to move at all, they are
forced to limp in concert.[142] Moreover, since a Christian man is sexually subject to his wife,[143] he is in effect trapped into sexual chastity.[144] No doubt this
seemed like a shocking form of bondage to many among
Chrysostom's readers, accustomed to a more relaxed sexual
standard for men.[145] Although the husband is the master
of the household, Chrysostom admits, what advantage is
this if he himself is enslaved?[146]

Developing Paul's notion of marriage as a "bond,"
Chrysostom fully exploits the pagan *topoi* on marriage.
As the latter brought home, marriage means that each
partner must put up with the other's faults. The husband
must endure his wife even if she is "wicked, carping, a
chatterbox, extravagant."[147] Unlike the pagan authors,
however, Chrysostom in these treatises stresses mostly
the woes of marriage that beset women, rather than those
that beset men—an approach no doubt conditioned by his
subject and his audience. He thus brings the trials of
marriage home to his female readers. If the wife dis-
covers that her husband has "morally depraved" desires,
she must nonetheless follow him.[148] Men may strike their
wives, cover them with abuse, subject them to the contempt of the servants: how many ways men have found to

punish their wives, Chrysostom exclaims![149]   The jealous
husband—a stock character in Chrysostom's analysis—encourages the servants to spy upon his wife's every deed,
word, yes, upon her every sigh. But if she tries to accuse him of wrongdoing, he will teach her to keep silent
fast enough. He can even have her executed, if he wishes,
Chrysostom notes.[150]   Inequality of economic status presents further problems in the relationship,[151] but even if
the two are on a par as far as property is concerned, the
potential equality is ruined by "the rule of subordination" in marriage, by which the wife is subject to her
husband.[152]

Next Chrysostom asks his readers to consider the
fears that attend the girl even before her husband is
picked. Will he suit her? What are his habits? Will
she please him? She is subject to the decision of her
father or guardian,[153] and becomes, in effect, the em-
barrassed subject of a financial transaction between two
men.[154] Next she must worry about childlessness, or con-
versely, about bearing too many children.[154] Even if a
child is safely born, after the pains and dangers of labor, its fate is a source of worry for years to come.[155]
A matron's entire life is spent in constant anxiety about
the death of loved ones—and her anticipated fear is as
difficult to bear as the grief resulting from an actual
death.[156] The problems occasioned by lazy, gossiping,
and vindictive servants illustrate still another disad-
vantage of marriage.[157]

The woes of second marriage are even more graphical-
ly depicted by Chrysostom. To all the problems of first
marriage are now added the hostilities and jealousies incumbent upon the new relationship. Step-children pose
special difficulties. Irrational jealousies toward the
spouse's dead partner prevail.[158] In particular does

Chrysostom dwell upon the suspicions that lurk in the mind
of the new husband as well as those of outsiders: how can
the woman be considered trustworthy, if she desecrated the
memory of her dead husband by marrying again?[159] What does
the second husband feel when he joins his bride on the marriage bed she shared with her first?[160] The new husband
always lives with the suspicion that he himself is being
scorned since the very fact that his wife remarried shows
her "faithlessness" to the man of her youth.[161] And, when
it comes to plain talk, Chrysostom reminds us that a man
can never love a widow in the frenzied passion with which
he embraces a virgin bride, for he always has in mind that
she has known another man.[162] Every husband, Chrysostom
insists, wants to think that he is his wife's "first and
only master (*kyrios*)."[163]

On the point of second marriage, Chrysostom, like
other Christian writers, follows the classical ideal of the
univira, the once-married woman. Despite changes in legis-
lation and mores during the Empire that granted more freedom to women, especially freedom of divorce, the traditional ideal of the monogamous woman was enshrined in literature as well as life.[164] From that pagan, especially Roman, ideal, Christian critics of second marriage such as
Tertullian and Jerome,[165] as well as Chrysostom, borrowed
much. Their denunciations of second marriage stand in contrast to Paul's timid suggestion that widows might, in his
opinion, be happier if they remained single.[166] Yet even
Paul's hesitant recommendation was not accepted by all New
Testament writers. The author of I Timothy, for example,
believed that younger widows should remarry, and that no
woman should be counted on the rolls of the church's widows
until she reached sixty years of age.[167]

Chrysostom's denunication of second marriage is, in
comparison, sharp. One might think, he argues, that widows

would have learned from hard experience the problems of
marriage and would not need guidance from him to encourage them to celibacy.[168] Widows who ponder remarriage
must suffer from amnesia regarding the conditions of marriage—unless, of course, they are motivated by desire
for worldly possessions, or worse yet, by "incontinence."[169] Only total inexperience with marriage could
explain why any female would seek it out,[170] and such inexperience a widow cannot claim. A monogamous woman has
at least exhibited a dignified self-control, but a woman
who remarries reveals that she has a "weak and carnal
soul."[171] In such ways does Chrysostom alter the values
of the earlier Christian tradition.

     In so depicting the woes of marriage, Chrysostom
undoubtedly meant to encourage his audience toward celibacy. He reminds them that virgins avoid all the afore-
mentioned problems: not only do they receive a higher
heavenly reward than the married, they also win the advantages of an unharried earthly life.[172] The virgin,
unlike the matron, has no worry except to present her
beautiful soul to her heavenly Bridegroom.[173] (The
Bridegroom Jesus, according to Chrysostom, accepts
celibate widows to himself as well.)[174] We might imagine,
given Chrysostom's emphasis on moral effort, that he
would concede to married people extra heavenly "credit"
for the trials they have endured in wedlock. Not so. In
the case of marriage, effort does not count, only the
triumph over evil, and celibates have a much keener edge
on achieving it, in Chrysostom's opinion.[175]

     Indeed, when the virgin contemplates the high re-
ward she will receive, her abstinence will be easy to
bear,[176] whatever her struggle may have been.[177] Of
course, Chrysostom asserts, she must have a pure soul as
well as a pure body:[178] decorum, devotion, and perfect

conduct are all essential to true virginity.[179] Those
who are merely bodily virgins but who have not exempli-
fied other Christian virtues—such as the foolish virgins
of Matthew 25 and probably the heretical ones as well—
will end up in hell.[180] Chrysostom is eager to insist
that mere externals, such as shabby clothing, cannot make
a true virgin.[181] Genuine Christian virgins must be completely unconcerned with worldly matters,[182] totally de-
tached from material affairs.[183] In this condition, the
virgin will be prepared to marry God and to receive the
wedding gifts of heaven.[184] The benefits of celibacy
thus provide a pleasing contrast to the woes of marriage.

In so describing the trials of marriage and the
glories of virginity, Chrysostom has gone far beyond his
Pauline source. The two treatises of Chrysostom that
follow are therefore no straightforward retelling of I
Corinthians 7. Christianity's entrance to the world of
"high" classical culture, its abandonment of an immediate
eschatological expectation, its struggle against Gnosti-
cizing heretics, its reflection on the origin and consequences of the Fall, its acceptance of gradation in moral
standards for Christians proportioned to their varying
degrees of religious commitment, all contributed to make
Chrysostom's commentary upon the Pauline chapter as much
an *eisegesis* as an *exegesis*.

NOTES

[1] The first recorded use of "Chrysostomos" for bishop John was in A.D. 553 by Pope Vigilius, *Constitutum Vigilii Papae de tribus capitulis* (PL 69, 101): "...Joannis Constantinopolitani episcopi, quem Chrysostomum vocant...." Of Chrysostom, the *Suda* reports, "...his tongue was more fluent than the cataracts of the Nile" (*Suidae Lexicon*, ed. Ada Adler [Leipzig: B. G. Teubner, 1931], II, 463 [p. 647, 31-32]).

[2] Aimé Puech, *Saint John Chrysostom, 344-407*. 2nd ed., tr. M. Partridge (London: R. and T. Washborne, Ltd., 1917), p. 3 (between A.D. 344 and 347); Anatole Moulard, *Saint Jean Chrysostome. Sa vie, son oeuvre* (Paris: Procure Générale du Clergé, 1941), p. 12 (A.D. 349); Chrysostomus Baur, *John Chrysostom and His Time*, tr. M. Gonzaga (Westminster, Md.: Newman Press, 1959), I, 3 (A.D. 354); Jean Dumortier, "La Valeur historique du Dialogue de Palladius et la chronologie de Saint Jean Chrysostome," *Mélanges de Science Religieuse* 7 (1951), 56 n.3. Dates in Chrysostom's early life as given by Robert E. Carter, "The Chronology of Saint John Chrysostom's Early Life," *Traditio* 18 (1962), 357-364 are: Chrysostom was born in A.D. 349, baptized in A.D. 368; spent A.D. 372-378 in ascetic retreat.

[3] Based on Palladius, *Dialogus de Vita S. Joannis Chrysostomi*, ed. P. R. Coleman-Norton (Cambridge: Cambridge University Press, 1928), V, 18 (p. 28).

[4] A. H. M. Jones, "St. John Chrysostom's Parentage and Education," *Harvard Theological Review* 46 (1953), 171.

[5] Socrates, *Historia ecclesiastica* VI, 3 (PG 67, 665); Sozomen, *Historia ecclesiastica* VIII, 2 (PG 67, 1513); Palladius reports that John Chrysostom's parents were *eugenōs* (*Dialogus* V, 18 [Coleman-Norton, p. 28]).

[6] John Chrysostom, *De sacerdotio* (PG 48, 624-625); *Ad viduam juniorem* 2 (PG 48, 601).

[7] Socrates, *Historia ecclesiastica* VI, 3 (PG 67, 665); Palladius, *Dialogus* V, 18 (Coleman-Norton, p. 28).

[8] Jones, "Chrysostom," p. 151.

[9]Socrates, *Historia ecclesiastica* VI, 3 (PG 67, 665);
Sozomen, *Historia ecclesiastica* VIII, 2 (PG 67, 1513).
Doubts on the relationship have been raised by Paul Petit,
Les Etudiants de Libanius (Paris: Nouvelles Editions
Latines, 1957), p. 41, and by A. J. Festugière, *Antioche
païenne et chrétienne: Libanius, Chrysostome et les
moines de Syrie* (Paris: Editions E. de Boccard, 1959),
pp. 409-410.

[10]Socrates, *Historia ecclesiastica* VI, 3 (PG 67,
665); Sozomen, *Historia ecclesiastica* VIII, 2 (PG 67,
1513).

[11]Paul Petit, *Libanius et la vie municipale à
Antioche au IVe siècle après J.-C.* (Paris: Librairie
Orientaliste Paul Geuthner, 1955), pp. 165-190; J. H. W. G.
Liebeschuetz, *Antioch: City and Imperial Administration
in the Later Roman Empire* (Oxford: Clarendon Press, 1972),
pp. 92-96; Glanville Downey, *Ancient Antioch* (Princeton:
Princeton University Press, 1963, chaps. 7-9. The sta-
tistic of 200,000 residents is based on John Chrysostom,
In S. Ignatium Martyrem (PG 50, 591). See Ausonius,
Ordo urbium nobilium XI, 4 for Antioch as equal to Alex-
andria.

[12]Petit, *Libanius,* pp. 191-216; Festugière *Antioche,*
passim; Liebeschuetz, *Antioch,* pp. 220, 227; Glanville
Downey, *A History of Antioch in Syria from Seleucus to
the Arab Conquest* (Princeton: Princeton University Press,
1961), pp. 447-450; Alain Natali, "Christianisme et cité
à Antioche à la fin du IVe siècle d'après Jean Chrysostome," in *Jean Chrysostome et Augustin: Actes du colloque
de Chantilly, 22-24 septembre 1974,* ed. Charles Kannengiesser (Paris: Editions Beauchesne, 1975), pp. 41-59;
Wayne A. Meeks and Robert L. Wilken, *Jews and Christians
in Antioch in the First Four Centuries of the Common Era*
(Missoula, Mont.: Scholars Press, 1978); C. H. Kraeling,
"The Jewish Community at Antioch," *Journal of Biblical
Literature* 51 (1932), 130-160. According to Chrysostom,
Christians at Antioch in his time numbered 100,000 per-
sons (*Hom. 85 Matt.* 4) (PG 58, 762).

[13]Downey, *A History of Antioch,* p. 351; E. S.
Bouchier, *A Short History of Antioch, 300 B.C.-A.D. 1268*
(Oxford: Basil Blackwell, 1921), pp. 146-147.

[14]Moulard, *Saint Jean Chrysostome. Sa vie,* p. 13;
Baur, *John Chrysostom* I, 85.

[15]Socrates, *Historia ecclesiastica* VI, 3 (PG 67,
665, 668); Sozomen, *Historia ecclesiastica* VIII, 2 (PG

67, 1516); John Chrysostom, *In Diodorum Tarsensem* (PG 52, 761-766). Festugière, *Antioche,* p. 183, writes that Diodore of Tarsus taught at Antioch from about 372-375.

[16]Socrates, *Historia ecclesiastica* VI, 3 (PG 67, 668); Sozomen, *Historia ecclesiastica* VIII, 2 (PG 67, 1516).

[17]Palladius, *Dialogus* V, 18 (Coleman-Norton, p. 28). On the development of monasticism in Syria, see Arthur Vööbus, *History of Asceticism in the Syrian Orient.* II: *Early Monasticism in Mesopotamia and Syria* (Louvain: CSCO, 1960); Pierre Canivet, *Le Monachisme syrien selon Théodoret de Cyr* (Paris: Editions Beauchesne, 1977), esp. chaps. 8-10; Jean Gribomont, "Le Monachisme au IVe s. en Asie Mineure: de Gangres au Messalianisme," *Studia Patristica* II (= *Texte und Untersuchungen* 64) (Berlin: Akademie-Verlag, 1957), 400-415; S. Jargy, "Les Premiers Instituts monastiques et les principaux répresentats du monachisme syrien au IVe siècle," *Proche Orient Chrétien* 4 (1954), 109-117. On Chrysostom and monasticism, see Jean-Marie Leroux, "Monachisme et communauté chrétienne d'après Saint Jean Chrysostome," *Théologie de la vie monastique,* vol. 49 (Paris: Aubier, 1961), 143-191, and "Saint Jean Chrysostome et le monachisme," in *Jean Chrysostome et Augustin,* ed. Kannengiesser, pp. 125-144; Ivo Auf der Maur, *Mönchtum und Glaubensverkündigung in den Schriften des hl. Johannes Chrysostomus* (Freiburg: Universitätsverlag, 1959).

[18]Palladius, *Dialogus* V, 18 (Coleman-Norton, p. 29).

[19]Palladius, *Dialogus* V, 18 (Coleman-Norton, p. 28); Baur, *John Chrysostom,* I, 85; Moulard, *Saint Jean Chrysostome. Sa vie,* p. 21.

[20]Palladius, *Dialogus* V, 19 (Coleman-Norton, p. 29); Socrates, *Historia ecclesiastica* VI, 3 (PG 67, 668). For a chronological summary, see Festugière, *Antioche,* pp. 413-414; Baur, *John Chrysostom,* I, 143; Moulard, *Saint Jean Chrysostome. Sa vie,* pp. 21, 30; Puech, *Saint John Chrysostom,* p. 16.

[21]According to Socrates, the following of Chrysostom's treatises were composed in Antioch (*Historia ecclesiastica* VI,3 [PG 67, 669]): *Against the Jews; On the Priesthood; Against Stagirius; On the Incomprehensibility of the Divine Nature; On the Women who Lived with Ecclesiastics.* For a discussion of Chrysostom's early ascetic treatises, including the modern dating of the two in this volume, see below, pp. ix-x.

[22]Socrates, Sozomen, Palladius devote most of their discussions of Chrysostom to his Constantinople period; the section of Theodoret's *Church History* on Chrysostom is entirely about his life in Constantinople.

[23]Palladius, *Dialogus* V, 19-20 (Coleman-Norton, pp. 31-33); XVIII, 62 (Coleman-Norton, pp. 112-113).

[24]Bernard Grillet, "Introduction générale," *John Chrysostome. La Virginité* (Paris: Les Editions du Cerf, 1966), p. 23; Moulard, *Saint Jean Chrysostome. Sa vie,* pp. 47-50; Baur, *John Chrysostom* I, 164-170.

[25]E.g., Bernard Grillet, "Introduction générale," *Jean Chrysostome. La Virginité,* pp. 67, 72; Bruno Vandenberghe, "St. Jean Chrysostome: pasteur des jeunes époux," *La Vie Spirituelle* 89 (1953), 39; Herbert Musurillo, "The Problem of Ascetical Fasting in the Greek Patristic Fathers," *Traditio* 12 (1956), 7-8.

[26]Carter, "Chronology," p. 371.

[27]The treatise is in PG 47, 387-392. See the discussion in Robert E. Carter, "Saint John Chrysostom's Rhetorical Use of the Socratic Distinction Between Kingship and Tyranny," *Traditio* 14 (1958), 368-369.

[28]*Comparatio potentiae, divitarum et excellentiae regis, cum monacho* 2 (PG 47, 389).

[29]*Comparatio* 4 (PG 47, 390-392).

[30]*Adversus oppognatores eorum qui vitam monasticam inducunt* II, 3; 9; 10 (PG 47, 335, 345, 346-347).

[31]*Adversus oppognatores* III, 8 (PG 47, 360-363); see Festugière, *Antioche,* pp. 195-208.

[32]*Ad viduam juniorem* (PG 48, 599-610).

[33]*Ad Theodorum lapsum* (PG 47, 277-316).

[34]According to Socrates, *Historia ecclesiastica* VI, 3 (PG 67, 669), one of the treatises was written in Antioch. Palladius, on the other hand, says the problem arose during Chrysostom's time in Constantinople (*Dialogus* V, 19 [Coleman-Norton, p. 31]). It has been suggested by Jean Dumortier, "La Date des deux traités de Sainte Jean Chrysostome aux moines et aux vierges," *Mélanges de Science Religieuse* 6 (1949), 251-252, that the two treatises were originally written in Antioch and re-issued in

Constantinople. The two treatises are *Adversus eos qui apud se habent virgines subintroductas* (PG 47, 495-514) and *Quod regulares feminae viris cohabitare non debeant* (PG 47, 513-532); English translation by Elizabeth A. Clark in *Jerome, Chrysostom, and Friends: Essays and Translations* (New York and Toronto: Edwin Mellen Press, 1979), pp. 158-248.

[35]Bernard Grillet's dating for the *De Virginitate* is around 382 A.D. ("Introduction générale," *Jean Chrysostome. La Virginité,*p. 25),against Herbert Musurillo's dating of the treatise to A.D. 392 ("Some Textual Problems in the Editing of the Greek Fathers," *Studia Patristica* III = Texte und Untersuchungen 78 [Berlin: Academie-Verlag, 1961], p. 92).

[36]Bernard Grillet, "Introduction générale," *Jean Chrysostome. A une jeune veuve. Sur le mariage unique* (Paris: Les Editions du Cerf, 1968), p. 14, dates *Against Remarriage* to between A.D. 383 and 386.

[37]Basil of Ancyra (=Pseudo-Athanasius), *De vera virginitate* (PG 28, 251-282); see also Michel Aubineau, "Les Ecrits de Saint Athanase sur le virginité," *Revue d'Ascétique et de Mystique* 31 (1955), 144-151.

[38]See David Amand de Mendieta, "La Virginité chez Eusèbe d'Emèse et l'ascéticisme familial dans la première moitié de IVe siècle," *Revue d'Histoire Ecclésiastique* 50 (1955), 790ff.

[39]See text in Michel Aubineau, ed., *Grégoire de Nysse. Traité de la virginité* (Paris: Les Editions du Cerf, 1966). Aubineau dates the treatise to A.D. 371 (p. 31).

[40]See Herbert Musurillo, "Introduction au texte grec," *Jean Chrysostome. La Virginité*, pp. 77-83, and Gerard H. Ettlinger, "Introduction au texte grec," *Jean Chrysostome. A une jeune veuve. Sur le mariage unique,* pp. 97-98.

[41]See notes 24 and 36 for bibliographical information.

[42]Grillet, "Introduction générale," *Jean Chrysostome. La Virginité,* p. 8.

[43]For discussion, see P. R. Coleman-Norton, "St. Chrysostom and the Greek Philosophers," *Classical Philology* 25 (1930), 305-317; Harry Hubbell, "Chrysostom and Rhetoric," *Classical Philology* 19 (1924), 261-276; Jean

Dumortier, "La Culture profane de S. Jean Chrysostome," *Mélanges de Science Religieuse* 10 (1953), 53-62; Anton Naegele, "Johannes Chrysostomos und sein Verhältnis zum Hellenismus," *Byzantinische Zeitschrift* 13 (1904), 73-113.

[44] I Corinthians 7:1-9, 25-40.

[45] I Corinthians 7:25-35.

[46] I Corinthians 7:28.

[47] *On Virginity* XXXIX, 1 (Musurillo, p. 228). English title and Roman numeration will be used hereafter, in accordance with Shore's translation.

[48] *On Virginity* XXXIX, 2 (Musurillo, pp. 228, 230).

[49] *Against Remarriage* 3 (Ettlinger, p. 174). English title will be used hereafter, in accordance with Shore's translation.

[50] See note 17 above for bibliography on early monasticism in Syria. The information about women's monasticism in fourth-century Syria is disappointingly thin: see Vööbus, *History of Asceticism,* II, 372.

[51] See note 38 above; for "home asceticism" in the West, see Elizabeth A. Clark, "Ascetic Renunciation and Feminine Advancement: A Paradox of Late Ancient Christianity," *Anglican Theological Review* 63 (1981), 240-257, and references therein.

[52] *Hom. 66 Matt.,* 3 (PG 58, 630).

[53] Grillet, "Introduction générale," *Jean Chrysostome. La Virginité,* p. 45: the treatise is addressed to those already converted to the virginal life.

[54] I Corinthians 7:25-29.

[55] The condemnation of the Montanist movement by second and third century writers is a case in point.

[56] *On Virginity* XLIX, 1-2 (Musurillo, pp. 274, 276).

[57] *On Virginity* XLIX, 5-6 (Musurillo, p. 280).

[58] *On Virginity* XLIX, 8 (Musurillo, p. 282).

[59] *Ibid.*

[60]*On Virginity* LXXIII, 3-4 (Musurillo, pp. 352, 354).

[61]*On Virginity* XI, 1 (Musurillo, p. 126): virginity makes angels out of us.

[62]*On Virginity* LIX (Musurillo, pp. 318, 320); *Against Remarriage* 6 (Ettlinger, p. 198). The virgin yearns for death because then she will see her Bridegroom face to face; the heretical virgins will not, because they are not betrothed to Christ (*On Virginity* I, 1 [Musurillo, p. 92]).

[63]Mark 12:25 = Matthew 22:30 = Luke 20:35-36.

[64]*On Virginity* XIV, 3; 5; 6 (Musurillo, pp. 140, 142).

[65]*On Virginity* XIV, 3 (Musurillo, p. 140).

[66]*On Virginity* XIV, 5; 6; XV, 2 (Musurillo, pp. 142, 146).

[67]Hesiod, *Works and Days* 197-200.

[68]*On Virginity* XIV, 5 (Musurillo, p. 142).

[69]*On Virginity* XIV, 6 (Musurillo, p. 142). Chrysostom's views on this topic echo those of Gregory of Nyssa. The view that marriage was not part of God's created order but the result of the Fall was strongly combatted by the Latin-writing theologian Augustine in a variety of treatises.

[70]*On Virginity* XIV, 6 (Musurillo, pp. 142, 144).

[71]*On Virginity* XV, 1 (Musurillo, p. 144).

[72]*On Virginity* XVIII (Musurillo, p. 156).

[73]*On Virginity* XIX, 1 (Musurillo, p. 156).

[74]John Chrysostom, *In propter fornicationes* 3 (PG 51, 213); *Hom. 20 Gen.* 1 (PG 53, 167); *Hom. 18 Gen.* 4 (PG 53, 154).

[75]*On Virginity* XIX, 1 (Musurillo, p. 156); I Corinthians 7:2, 8-9, 36.

[76]*On Virginity* XIX, 1 (Musurillo, p. 158).

[77]*On Virginity* XV, 2 (Musurillo, p. 146).

[78]*On Virginity* XIX, 2 (Musurillo, p. 158); IX, 1 (Musurillo, p. 120); marriage is compared with a dam that contains the flood of sexual desire.

[79]*On Virginity* XIX, 2 (Musurillo, p. 158).

[80]*On Virginity* XVI, 1; 2 (Musurillo, pp. 146, 148); XVII, 1-2; 5 (Musurillo, pp. 150, 154).

[81]I Corinthians 13:11.

[82]I Corinthians 3:1-2; also see Hebrews 5:12-13.

[83]*On Virginity* XLIV, 1 (Musurillo, pp. 250, 252).

[84]*On Virginity* LXXXIV, 1 (Musurillo, p. 390); LXXXIII, 1-2 (Musurillo, pp. 386, 388). For some positive themes in Chrysostom's evaluation of marriage, see T. Špidlík, "Il matrimonio, sacramento di unità, nel pensiero di Crisostomo," *Augustinianum* 17 (1977), 221-226; and Anatole Moulard, *Saint Jean Chrysostome. Le Défenseur du mariage et l'apotre de la virginité* (Paris: Librairie Victor Lecoffre, 1923), esp. pt. I, chaps. 2-5.

[85]For example, Clement of Alexandria, *Stromateis* III; Jerome, *Epp.* 22, 13; 48, 2; 133, 9; *Adversus Jovinianus* I, 3.

[86]Unless one takes the Corinthian enthusiasts as outright Gnostics and attributes to them the sentiment of I Cor. 7:1: "It is better for a man not to touch a woman." See C. K. Barrett, *A Commentary on the First Epistle to the Corinthians* (London: Adam and Charles Black, 1968), pp. 154-155; John C. Hurd, Jr., *The Origin of I Corinthians* (New York: Seabury Press, 1965), pp. 154-163. On the Gnostic question, see Walter Schmithals, *Gnosticism in Corinth,* tr. J. E. Steely (Nashville: Abingdon Press, 1971), and *Paul and the Gnostics,* tr. J. E. Steely (Nashville: Abingdon Press, 1972).

[87]I Timothy 4:3; Matt. 19:10-12 and Col. 2:23 suggest an ascetic movement as well.

[88]See note 85 above and Hans Jonas, *Gnosis und Spätantiker Geist* (Göttingen: Vandenhoeck & Ruprecht, 1964), I, 233-238; J. P. Broudéhoux, *Mariage et famille chez Clément d'Alexandrie* (Paris: Beauchesne, 1970), pp. 27-61.

[89]*On Virginity* III (Musurillo, pp. 100, 102); II, 1

(Musurillo, p. 98).

[90]*On Virginity* II, 2 (Musurillo, p. 100); IV, 2 (Musurillo, p. 104).

[91]*On Virginity* V, 1 (Musurillo, p. 106).

[92]*On Virginity* VIII, 1 (Musurillo, p. 114).

[93]*On Virginity* I, 2 (Musurillo, pp. 92, 94); II, 2 (Musurillo, p. 100); VIII, 3 (Musurillo, p. 116).

[94]*On Virginity* I, 3 (Musurillo, p. 94).

[95]*On Virginity* X, 1 (Musurillo, p. 122).

[96]*Ibid.*

[97]Moulard, *Saint Jean Chrysostome. Le Défenseur,* pt. I, chap. 3.

[98]See especially Robin Scroggs, "Paul and the Eschatological Woman," *Journal of the American Academy of Religion* 40 (1972), 283-303; Elaine H. Pagels, "Paul and Women: A Response to Recent Discussion," *Journal of the American Academy of Religion* 42 (1974), 538-549; more recently see Raoul Mortley, *Womanhood. The Feminine in Ancient Hellenism, Gnosticism, Christianity, and Islam* (Sydney: Delacroix Press, 1981), pp. 45-54.

[99]Romans 5:12-14, 18-19. But see II Corinthians 11:3.

[100]E.g., I Timothy 2:14; *On Virginity* XLVI, 1 (Musurillo, p. 258).

[101]*On Virginity* XLVI, 1 (Musurillo, pp. 256, 258).

[102]*On Virginity* XLVI, 2 (Musurillo, p. 258).

[103]*Ibid.*

[104]Genesis 2:18; *On Virginity* XLVI, 1 (Musurillo, p. 256).

[105]*On Virginity* XLVI, 5 (Musurillo, pp. 260, 262).

[106]*On Virginity* XLVI, 5 (Musurillo, p. 262).

[107]*On Virginity* XLVII, 2 (Musurillo, p. 266).

[108]*On Virginity* LII, 2-7 (Musurillo, pp. 288, 290,

292, 295, 296, 298); LVI, 1 (Musurillo, p. 304); LVII,
1-7 (Musurillo, pp. 308, 310, 312, 314); LXVII (Musurillo,
pp. 336, 338); and especially XL, 3 (Musurillo, p. 234).
There is never equality in marriage, whatever the woman's
economic situation: *On Virginity* LV (Musurillo, p. 302).

[109]See, for example, *Hom. 8 Rom.* 1 (PG 60, 455); *Hom.
10 Rom.* 3 (PG 60, 473); *Hom. 10 Rom.* 5 (PG 60, 480); *Hom.
3 Phil.* 1 (PG 52, 197).

[110]*On Virginity* LXIII, 3 (Musurillo, p. 328).

[111]*On Virginity* LXX, 1-2 (Musurillo, p. 346); LXXI
(Musurillo, pp. 346, 348). Also see Chrysostom's *Comparatio* for similar arguments concerning the superiority
of a monk's life to a king's.

[112]See A. Uleyn, "La Doctrine morale de S. Jean
Chrysostome dans le Commentaire sur S. Matthieu et ses
affinités avec la diatribe," *Revue de l'Université
d'Ottawa* 27 (1957), 103-105, 120-136.

[113]See especially Louis Meyer, "Liberté et moralisme
chretién dans la doctrine spirituelle de Saint Jean
Chrysostome," *Recherches de Science Religieuse* 23 (1933),
283-305.

[114]*On Virginity* LXXVII, 6 (Musurillo, p. 374).

[115]*On Virginity* VIII, 3 (Musurillo, p. 116).

[116]E.g., V. J. Stiglmayr, "Zur Aszese des heiligen
Chrysostomus" *Zeitschrift für Aszese und Mystik* 4 (1929),
38-39; Meyer, "Liberté," p. 295.

[117]*On Virginity* XXXVI, 1-3 (Musurillo, pp. 212, 214,
216).

[118]*On Virginity* XXXV, 2 (Musurillo, p. 210).

[119]A phrase from Stoic ethics often used by Chrysostom. See Anne-Marie Malingrey, "Introduction," *Jean
Chrysostome. Lettres à Olympias. Vie anonyme d'Olympias.*
2nd ed. (Paris: Les Editions du Cerf, 1968), p. 54.

[120]*On Virginity* XXXIX, 3 (Musurillo, p. 230).

[121]*On Virginity* LXXXIV, 3-4 (Musurillo, pp. 392,
394).

[122]*On Virginity* LXXVI, 1 (Musurillo, p. 364).

[123]*Against Remarriage* 6 (Ettlinger, p. 194).

[124]*On Virginity* XXXIX, 1-2 (Musurillo, pp. 228, 230).

[125]*On Virginity* XXXVIII, 1-2 (Musurillo, p. 226).

[126]So called from the wording of Matthew 19:21, "If you would be perfect...." See C. Baur, "Der Weg der Vollkommenheit nach dem heiligen Joh. Chrysostomus," *Theologie und Glaube* 20 (1928), 27, 37; Louis Meyer, "Perfection chrétienne et vie solitaire dans la pensée des St. Jean Chrysostome." *Revue d'Ascetique et de Mystique* 14 (1933), 234. For an argument against Chrysostom having a two-tiered morality, see C. Baur, "Das Ideal der christlichen Vollkommenheit nach dem hl. Johannes Chrysostomus," *Theologie und Glaube* 6 (1914), 573-574; Stiglmayr, "Zur Aszese," pp. 40-41, 46.

[127]See, for example, *On Virginity* L, 1-2 (Musurillo, pp. 284, 286); LXXXII, 4 (Musurillo, p. 386).

[128]Jerome's interpretation of the parable of the sower provides a particularly apt illustration of this point. The "100-fold harvest" he takes to mean the reward awaiting virgins, the "60-fold harvest" is that the widows will receive, while married people can expect only the "30-fold harvest": *Against Jovinian* I, 3; *Ep.* 48, 2.

[129]*On Virginity* II, 2 (Musurillo, p. 100).

[130]*On Virginity* I, 1 (Musurillo, p. 92).

[131]*On Virginity* I, 2-3 (Musurillo, pp. 94, 96).

[132]*On Virginity* VIII, 3 (Musurillo, p. 116).

[133]*On Virginity* XXX, 2 (Musurillo, p. 192).

[134]*On Virginity* VIII, 5 (Musurillo, p. 118).

[135]I Corinthians 12:4-31. For Chrysostom's understanding of the *charismata,* see Adolf Martin Ritter, *Charisma im Verständnis des Johannes Chrysostomos und seiner Zeit* (Göttingen: Vandenhoeck & Ruprecht, 1972), pp. 53-98.

[136]I Corinthians 7:7.

[137]See Malingrey, "Introduction," p. 54. On *prohairesis,* see Edward Nowak, *Le Chrétien devant la*

souffrance. *Etude sur la pensée de Jean Chrysostome* (Paris: Beauchesne, 1972), pp. 57-63.

[138] I Corinthians 7:3-4.

[139] I Corinthians 7:32-34.

[140] For Chrysostom's use of the *topoi* on marriage, see Moulard, *Saint Jean Chrysostome. Le Défenseur*, pp. 202-217; Grillet, "Introduction générale," *A une jeune veuve. Sur le mariage unique,* pp. 76-77; and Leroux, "Monachisme," pp. 155, 165; for Gregory of Nyssa's use of similar *topoi* and references, see Aubineau, *Grégoire de Nysse. Traité de la Virginité*, pp. 87-96.

[141] *On Virginity* XXVIII, 3 (Musurillo, p. 184), XL, 1 (Musurillo, p. 232).

[142] *On Virginity* XLI, 2 (Musurillo, pp. 236, 238).

[143] *On Virginity* XLI, 2 (Musurillo, p. 236); XXVIII, 1 (p. 182).

[144] *On Virginity* XXVIII, 1 (Musurillo, p. 182); XXXII, 3 (Musurillo, p. 196).

[145] See Derrick Sherwin Bailey, *Sexual Relation in Christian Thought* (New York: Harper and Row, 1959), p. 11.

[146] *On Virginity* XLI, 2 (Musurillo, p. 236).

[147] *On Virginity* XL, 1 (Musurillo, p. 232).

[148] *On Virginity* XLVII, 5 (Musurillo, p. 270).

[149] *On Virginity* XL, 2-3 (Musurillo, p. 234).

[150] *On Virginity* LII, 1-7 (Musurillo, pp. 228, 290, 292, 294, 296). Certainly the right of a husband to murder his complaining wife with impunity did not exist in Chrysostom's time. Supposedly before the issuance of *lex Julia de Adulteriis,* between 18 and 16 B.C., a husband who caught his wife in an act of adultery could execute her on the spot, without benefit of trial (so Aulus Gellius, *Noctes Atticae* 10, 23, 5). But even by the first century B.C., *manus* marriage was passing away in favor of freer forms that gave the husband less absolute power over his wife. Chrysostom, here as elsewhere, appeals to older customs. See Percy E. Corbett, *The Roman*

Law of Marriage (Oxford: Clarendon Press, 1930), pp. 127-135.

[151]*On Virginity* LIII-LV (Musurillo, pp. 298, 300, 302).

[152]*On Virginity* LV (Musurillo, p. 302).

[153]*On Virginity* LVII, 1-2 (Musurillo, pp. 308, 310).

[154]*On Virginity* LVII, 3 (Musurillo, p. 310).

[155]*On Virginity* LVII, 5 (Musurillo, pp. 312, 314).

[156]*On Virginity* LVI, 1-2 (Musurillo, pp. 304, 306).

[157]*On Virginity* LXVII (Musurillo, pp. 336, 338).

[158]*On Virginity* XXXVII, 3 (Musurillo, pp. 220, 222); *Against Remarriage* 2 (Ettlinger, p. 170); 6 (Ettlinger, p. 192).

[159]*On Virginity* XXXVII, 1 (Musurillo, p. 218).

[160]*Against Remarriage* 2 (Ettlinger, p. 170).

[161]*Against Remarriage* 6 (Ettlinger, p. 192).

[162]*Against Remarriage* 5 (Ettlinger, pp. 188, 190).

[163]*Against Remarriage* 5 (Ettlinger, p. 190).

[164]See, for example, discussions and examples in Gordon Williams, "Some Aspects of Roman Marriage Ceremonies and Ideals," *Journal of Roman Studies* 48 (1958), 16-29; Marjorie Lightman and William Zeisel, "Univira: An Example of Continuity and Change in Roman Society," *Church History* 46 (1977), 19-32.

[165]For their attacks on remarriage, see especially Tertullian, *De exhortatione castitatis* and *De monogamia;* Jerome *Epp.* 54; 79; 123.

[166]I Corinthians 7:39-40.

[167]I Timothy 5:9-14.

[168]*Against Remarriage* 5 (Ettlinger, p. 188).

[169]*Against Remarriage* 1 (Ettlinger, p. 162).

[170]*Against Remarriage* 1 (Ettlinger, p. 160); 5 (Ettlinger, p. 188).

[171]*Against Remarriage* 2 (Ettlinger, p. 168).

[172]*On Virginity* XLIX, 8 (Musurillo, p. 282); LII, 8 (Musurillo, p. 284); LXV (Musurillo, p. 332).

[173]*On Virginity* LIX (Musurillo, pp. 318, 320); LX, 1 (Musurillo, p. 320).

[174]*Against Remarriage* 6 (Ettlinger, pp. 196, 198).

[175]*On Virginity* XLV, 1 (Musurillo, pp. 254, 256). Thus the heretical virgins will find that their effort has not counted; their virginity resulted from the wrong motivation (*On Virginity* IV, 3 [Musurillo, pp. 104, 106)].

[176]*On Virginity* LXIV (Musurillo, p. 330).

[177]*On Virginity* XXXIV, 1 (Musurillo, pp. 198, 200); 4 (Musurillo, p. 202).

[178]*On Virginity* V, 2 (Musurillo, p. 108); VI, 1 (Musurillo, p. 108).

[179]*On Virginity* LXXX, 2 (Musurillo, p. 380).

[180]*On Virginity* LXXXII, 3 (Musurillo, p. 384); cf. Chrysostom's comments on the "foolish virgins" of Matthew 25 in *Vidua eligatur* 15 (PG 51, 336); *Hom. 78 Matt.* (PG 58, 711-718).

[181]*On Virginity* VII, 1-2 (Musurillo, p. 112).

[182]*On Virginity* LXXVII (Musurillo, p. 366).

[183]*On Virginity* LXVIII (Musurillo, pp. 338, 340, 342).

[184]*On Virginity* LIX (Musurillo, pp. 318, 320.

JOHN CHRYSOSTOM

--ON VIRGINITY

--AGAINST REMARRIAGE

Translation by Sally Rieger Shore

ON VIRGINITY

I
The Virginity Of The Heretics Has No Reward

1. The Jews disdain the beauty of virginity, and this is not astonishing because they have dishonored Christ himself, born of a virgin. The Greeks admire it in amazement, but only the Church of God praises it. But the heretical virgins[1] I could never call virgins, first of all because they are not chaste; they have not been betrothed to one man as the apostle of Christ, the leader of the bride, wishes when he says: "I have given you in marriage to one husband, presenting you as a chaste virgin to Christ."[2] Even if this was said about the entire assembly of the Church, nevertheless, the phrase has relevance for the virgins too. Therefore, how could they be chaste who unsatisfied with one husband introduce another who is not God?

2. This is the first reason why they could not be virgins. The second is that they have dishonored marriage and in this way have come to the abstention from it. By decreeing that marriage is bad, they have robbed themselves of the prizes of virginity in advance, for it would only be just, not that those who refrain from evil win a crown for this, but rather that they not be punished. These same principles are exhibited not only by us but

also in the laws drawn up in pagan society. "Put the
murderer to death," their law says. There is no corol-
lary: "Honor him who does not murder." "Punish the thief,"
their law says, but there is no further command that he
who is not a thief receive a gift. If they condemn to
death the adulterer, they do not regard him who does not
disrupt the marriages of others as worthy of any honor.
This is very reasonable; for commendation and admiration
belong   to those who successfully bring about good and
not to those who avoid evil. There is sufficient satisfaction for the latter in not experiencing any punishment.

3. For this reason too our Lord has threatened the
penalty of hell if someone impulsively and without cause
grows angry with his brother and calls him a fool.[3] But
he did not promise the kingdom of heaven to those who do
not grow angry without cause and refrain from abusive language; instead he required something more than this, something greater when he said: "Love your enemies."[4] He
wanted to show that not hating one's brother is a very
small and paltry thing, worthy of no honor. Although he
established what is far more worthwhile as a goal, namely,
brotherly love and affection, he did not say that even
such action on our part is sufficient to win us any honor.
How could it, when we are no more virtuous in this than
the Gentiles?[5] So we need some other additional qualifi-
cation, greater than this, if we intend to demand a wage.
Do not now think, our Lord says, you are worthy of a
crown because I do not condemn you to hell for refraining
from insults and anger directed at your brother. I do not
require just that much goodness. No, even if in addition
to not insulting him you say you love him, still you will
be returned to a lower place and be ranked near the tax-
collectors.[6] But if you wish to be perfect and worthy of
heaven, do not stop at this point but climb further up

and grasp a philosophy surpassing nature itself; and this
is to love your enemies.

4. Therefore, since we generally agree on this
point, let the heretics stop beating themselves in vain,
for they will get no wage for it—not because the Lord is
unjust, far from it, but because they themselves are ignorant and wicked. In what way? It has been shown that
there is no gift in store for the mere avoidance of wickedness, but they eschew marriage on the grounds that it is
bad; and so, how could they demand a wage for their with-
drawal from it? Just as we will not think ourselves
worthy of a crown for not committing adultery, so neither
could they for not marrying. On the day of judgment the
judge will say to them: "I have not fixed honors for those
who have merely refrained from evil (for this is trivial
in my opinion), but all those who have practiced virtue,
these I bring to the eternal inheritance of heaven." And
so, if you think marriage is impure and accursed, how
could you demand in return for your avoidance of it the
prizes that are in store for those who practice virtue?

5. This is why Christ places his sheep on his
right[7] and with praises leads them into his kingdom, not
because they have not stolen the property of others, but
because they have distributed to others their own goods.
And he gladly accepts the man who was entrusted with five
talents, not because he did not diminish the sum, but because he increased the sum loaned and gave back twice as
much.[8] When, therefore, will you stop running about in
circles and tiring yourself in vain, as you wildly punch
and shadow-box.[9] And I wish it were just a matter of
running about in circles. This is not a trivial matter,
however, if we consider the penalty, for those who work
hard and expect many greater prizes for their efforts

have been ranked on the day of judgment among the dishonored.

II
The Heretics Are Even Punished
For Their Practice Of Virginity

1. This is not the only dire result of their action and their punishment is not limited to the gains
they did not make. Other penalties much more severe will
await them: the fire that is never extinguished, the worm
that dies not,[10] the darkness outside,[11] the affliction
and anguish.[12] So we need a thousand mouths and the power
of angels to return to God the thanks that is worthy of
his solicitude for us. Yet it is not possible even in
this way. How could it be? For the effort required by
virginity is the same for us and the heretics, and perhaps
it is much greater for them. The fruit of the efforts,
however, is not the same. For them it means fetters,
tears, lamentations and unending punishment; for us it is
the destiny of the angels, bright torches, and the sum
total of all goodness: life with the bridegroom.

2. Why are the wages for the same efforts so different? It is because they have chosen virginity to oppose the law of God, whereas we practice it to accomplish
his will. He who has Christ speaking within him testi-
fies that God wishes all men to refrain from marriage:
"I should like you," he says, "to be as I am," that is,
continent.[13] Since the Savior spares us and knows that
"the spirit is willing but nature is weak,"[14] he has not
forced the issue by laying down a command but has entrusted the choice to our souls. If there had been a
command and law, the upright would not have been able to
enjoy honor but would have heard Christ say: "You have
done what you ought to;" and those who failed would not

have obtained pardon but would pay the penalty fixed for
those who act unlawfully. When he says: "Let him accept
this teaching who can,"[15] he does not condemn those who
cannot, but to those who are capable he points out the
supernatural nature of the contest. For this reason Paul,
too, following in the steps of his Master says: "I have
not received any commandment from the Lord, but give my
own opinion."[16]

III
Their Abhorrence Of Marriage
Is A Sign Of Satanic Inhumanity

But neither Marcion nor Valentinus nor Mani main-
tained this moderate view. They did not have speaking in
themselves the Christ who spares his own sheep and who
lays down his life for them but instead the father of
falsehood, the destroyer of the human race.[17] Consequently, they have destroyed all their followers by oppressing
them in this world with meaningless and unbearable tasks
and by dragging them down in their wake into the fire prepared for them in the next world.

IV
The Heretics Observing Virginity
Are More Pitiable Than The Pagans

1. Oh, you are more wretched than the pagans! For
even if the horrors of hell await them, nevertheless the
pagans here and now at least enjoy the pleasures of life;
they marry, enjoy what money buys and indulge themselves
in other ways. Yet for you there is torture and hardship
in both worlds: in this one when you are willing, in the
next when you are not. No one will reward the pagans for
fasting and practicing virginity, but neither is punishment in store for them. You, on the other hand, instead

of receiving the multitude of praises you were expecting
will pay the supreme penalty. With the other sinners you
will hear: "Out of my sight...into the everlasting fire
prepared for the devil and his angels,"[18] because you
fasted and practiced virginity.

2. For fasting and virginity are neither good nor
evil in themselves but from the purpose of those who practice them comes each of these qualities. The practice of
this virtue is unprofitable for the pagans; they earn no
wage because they did not pursue it out of fear of God.
As for you, because you fight with God and slander the
objects of his creation, not only will you go unrewarded,
you will even be punished. You will be ranked with the
pagans for your opinions since you have denied as they do
the true God and have introduced polytheism. Yet they
will fare better than you because of their way of life.
Their penalty will be limited to not receiving any good,
but for you there will be the additional punishment of
suffering evil. While it was possible for them to enjoy
everything in the present life, you will be deprived both
now and later.

3. Is there any punishment more severe than receiving penalties in exchange for one's work and sweat?
The adulterer, the covetous, those treating the possessions of others with contempt and the thief preying on
his neighbor[19] have some consolation, although it is
short-lived; nevertheless, their punishment is for the
sins they enjoyed in this world. On the other hand, he
who submits voluntarily to poverty to be rich in the next
world and endures the hardships of virginity to join in
the chorus of angels is suddenly and unexpectedly punished for the very behavior that he hoped would be to his
advantage. It is impossible to say how much suffering he
endures because of this unexpected outcome. I think, in

fact, that he is tortured as much by hell's fire as by
the knowledge that those who had made similar efforts are
in the presence of Christ while he pays the supreme penalty for doing what earned for them ineffable good. He is
tormented when he realizes that, although he has spent
his life devoted to chastity, he suffers harsher punishments than the dissolute and lascivious.

V
The Virginity Of The Heretics
Is Even More Impure Than Adultery

1. Indeed, the chastity of the heretics is worse
than all profligacy, which limits its wrongs to injuries
against men; their chastity however quarrels with God and
insults his boundless wisdom. The devil has fixed such
snares for those who serve him. It is not my theory that
the virginity of the heretics is specifically the inven-
tion of the devil's wickedness.

2. What then does Paul say? "The Spirit distinct-
ly says that in later times some will turn away from the
faith and will heed deceitful spirits and things taught
by demons through plausible liars—men with seared con-
sciences who forbid marriage and require abstinence from
foods which God created to be received...by believers
...."[20] In what way then is she a virgin who has fallen
away from the faith, who has devoted herself to the de-
ceivers, who obeys the demons and honors falsehood? In
what way is she a virgin who has a seared conscience?
For the virgin must be pure not only in body but also in
soul if she is going to receive the holy bridegroom. How
could this woman be pure with so many scars? If it is
necessary to banish mortal cares from this bridal chamber,
since it is not possible to be presentable[21] in their company, how will she be able to preserve the beauty of

virginity when she has unholy thoughts within?

VI
The Heretics Who Practice Virginity Defile
Not Only Their Souls But Also Their Bodies

1.   Even if her body should remain inviolate the better part of her soul has been ruined: her thoughts. What advantage is there in the walls having stood firm when the temple has been destroyed? Or what good is it that the place where the throne stood is pure when the throne itself is defiled?[22] No, not in this way has her body escaped pollution. Blasphemy and evil words are produced within but they do not stay there; they defile the tongue when uttered by the mouth, and one's hearing, which receives them. It is similar to deleterious drugs attacking the heart: they gnaw through its roots more savagely than any worm and destroy the rest of the body along with the heart. If, then, virginity is defined by holiness of body and soul, but a woman is unholy and impure in each respect, how could she be a virgin? —But she shows me a pale face, wasted limbs, a shabby garment, and gentle glance. —What is the good of all that when the eye of the soul is bold,[23] for what could be more audacious than that eye encouraging her real eyes to consider the objects of God's creation as bad?

2.   "All the glory of the daughter of the king is within."[24] The heretical virgin has reversed the meaning of this expression by wearing the glory on the exterior but being entirely dishonored within. It is criminal to display before men extreme modesty but to employ with God, who created her, great folly. Although she does not dare to look man in the face—if there is any such woman among the heretics—she looks with impudent eyes at the Master of men, and shouts her wrongdoing to the skies. —Their faces are wooden, you say, like a corpse. —This is why they deserve

tears and much lamentation, because they have taken upon
themselves so much hardship without purpose and to their
own peril.

VII
We Must Judge Virginity On The Basis
Of One's Soul, Not One's Clothing

1.   You say that her clothes are shabby, but virginity resides not in clothing nor in one's complexion
but in the body and soul. Is it not strange that we have
different standards? We will not judge the philosopher
by his hair or his staff or his tunic, but by his way of
life, his character and soul; the soldier too we will not
approve for his mantle or belt but for his strength and
manliness; yet the virgin, who represents a state so admirable and superior to all others, we will simply and
offhandedly assume practices her virtue because of the
squalor of her hair, her dejected look and grey cloak.
We do not strip her soul bare and scrutinize closely its
inner state.

2.   But he who has drawn up the rules for this contest does not permit this. He orders that those who have
entered not be judged by their clothing but by the con-
victions of their souls. "Athletes," Paul says, "deny
themselves all sorts of things,"[25] all that troubles the
health of the soul; and "if one takes part in an athletic
contest, he cannot receive the winner's crown unless he
has kept the rules."[26] What, then, are the laws of this
contest? Hear again his words, or rather Christ himself,
who has established the contest: "The virgin is concerned
with things of the Lord, in pursuit of holiness in body
and spirit;"[27] and again, "Let marriage be honored and
the marriage bed be kept undefiled."[28]

VIII
It Is Prejudicial For The Virgin
To Be Arrogant With Married People

1.   ──What has this to do with me, you say, since I
have said farewell to marriage? ──This, poor woman, this
has been your undoing: that you think the doctrine of
marriage is of no concern to you. By treating marriage
with excessive contempt and acting insolently toward God's
wisdom, you have slandered all his creation. For if marriage is impure, all living things begotten by it are im-
pure──not to mention human nature. How, then, can an impure maiden be a virgin? For this is the second, rather
third, kind of defilement and impurity you have thought
of. Women who avoid marriage as an accursed institution
by this very act become more accursed than everyone and
find that virginity is more abominable than fornication.

2.   With whom, then, will we rank you? The Jews?
But they do not allow this practice; they, in fact, honor
marriage and marvel at God's creation. Will we rank you
with us? But you do not hear Christ speaking through
Paul: "Let marriage be honored in every way and the marriage bed be kept undefiled."[29] What is left? To rank
you with the pagans? But even they will reject you for
being unholier than they. For Plato says that "he was
good who made all of this," and that "no envy over anything is born in what is good."[30] In contrast, you call
God wicked and the creator of wicked works. But do not
be alarmed; you have the devil and his angels sharing in
this opinion──but no, not his angels; for although they
have inspired you to such madness, do not think they
themselves are like-minded. They know that God is good.
Hear them shouting first this: "We know who you are, the
holy one of God,"[31] and now, "These men are the servants
of the Most High God; they will make known to you a way
of salvation."[32]

3.   Will you still speak of virginity and pride
yourself for it?   When you die, will you not weep for
yourselves and lament your folly, through which the devil
binds you just as captives and drags you into the fire of
hell?   You did not enter into marriage?   This is not the
only criterion for virginity.   For I would call the woman
who has the power to marry but chooses not to a virgin.
By saying that marriage is forbidden, virtuous action becomes no longer a matter of deliberate choice but an obligation to obey the law.   For this reason, we admire the
Persians for not marrying their mothers, but not the Romans.   Among the Romans, such a marriage is thought to be
a loathsome act by all, without exception; but in Persia,
since people dared this practice with impunity, those ab-
staining from such intercourse deserved praise.
4.   There must be a close examination of marriage
along the same lines.   Since our custom is to allow everyone to marry, we naturally admire those who do not; but
you, by thrusting it into an inferior rank, could not now
claim praise for your continence.   To abstain from what
has been forbidden is by no means the mark of a noble and
generous soul.   Perfect virtue does not consist of not
doing those things for which we would think ourselves
wicked before everyone.   It consists of excelling in what
does not entail reproach for those who do not choose it.
It not only preserves those who have successfully elected
this course from a bad reputation, it also admits them into the rank of the good.
5.   Just as no one would praise eunuchs for virginity because they do not marry, so no one would praise you.
What has been for them a natural constraint is for you a
stratagem of your perverted conscience.   And just as the
mutilation of their bodies deprives eunuchs of distinction in this virtue, so the devil by cutting off your up-

right thoughts (although you remain intact outwardly) com-
pels you not to marry, thereby causing you pain but allowing you no honors. Do you forbid marriage? Then no wage
for not marrying will be in store for you. Instead there
will be retribution and punishment.

IX
To Advise Virginity Is
Not To Forbid Marriage

1. —You will say, "Do *you* not forbid it?"   —Non-
sense! may I never rave as you do. —"Why then do you encourage us not to marry?" —Because I believe virginity
is much more honorable than marriage. I do not of course
count marriage among evil things, rather I praise it exceedingly. It is the harbor of chastity for those who desire to use it well, and it does not allow one's nature to
become wild. For like a dam, marriage gives us an opportunity for legitimate intercourse and in this way contains
the flood of sexual desire. It deposits us in a calm sea
and watches over us. But there are some who do not need
this security; instead, by fasting, vigils, sleeping on
the ground, and the practice of other hardships, they tame
the madness of their nature. These I advise not to marry
but I do not forbid it.

2. There is a great difference between these two
philosophies, as great a difference as that between necessity and choice. In the one case, the adviser gives the
listener a choice; in the other, the listener is deprived
of this decision. Besides, when I recommend virginity, I
do not bring discredit to marriage or denounce one for not
obeying. You, however, slander marriage by saying it is
of no consequence. You seize the role of legislator and
not that of adviser, and, as is to be expected, hate those
who do not obey. But I do not. Instead, I admire those

who enroll for this contest, but I do not accuse those who
decline to do so.

3. An accusation would be justified if someone inclines toward a commonly acknowledged evil. But the man
who displays a lesser good and who does not aim at what is
better, although he has forfeited praise for the higher
virtue, would not be justly denounced. How then can I
forbid marriage if I do not accuse those who do marry? I
forbid fornication and adultery but marriage never. I also punish those venturing the former acts and expel them
from the assembly of the church, but I continuously praise
those who marry if they are chaste. So there are two advantages in my position: first, not slandering the work of
God; second, not diminishing the dignity of virginity but
demonstrating that it is much more worthy of respect.

X

The Detractor Of Marriage
Does Harm To Virginity

1. The detractor of marriage also reduces the glory
of virginity, whereas one who praises marriage increases
admiration for it and makes it more magnificent. For what
appears good in comparison with something inferior would
not be very good; but that which is better than what is
acknowledged as good is exceedingly good, the very thing
we show virginity to be. Therefore, even as the detractors
of marriage tarnish the eulogies for virginity, so he who
removes marriage from censure has not recommended it over
virginity. The same is true with human bodies: those are
better that have not been maimed, that are sound and without injury; these we call beautiful.

2. Is marriage a good? Then virginity is admirable
because it is better than a good, as much better as a
helmsman is than his sailors, and a general than his army.

But even as on a ship, if you remove the rowers, you dis-
able the ship, and as in war, if you cause the soldiers to
revolt, you bind up and surrender the general to the enemy,
so too in this case, if you banish marriage from the position of honor, you betray the glory of virginity and place
it in extreme danger.

      3. Is virginity a good? Yes, I fully agree. But
is it better than marriage? I agree with this, too. If
you wish, I will illustrate the difference like this: virginity is as much superior to marriage as heaven is to
earth, as the angels are to men, and, to use far stronger
language, it is more superior still. For the angels, if
they do not marry and are not given in marriage,[33] are not
a mixture of flesh and blood. They do not pass time on
earth and endure trouble from the passions. They require
neither food nor drink. Sweet song cannot appease them,
nor can a radiant face win them over, nor any other such
thing. Their natures of necessity remain transparent and
brilliant, with no passion troubling them, like the
heavens at high noon clear and undisturbed by any cloud.

XI
Virginity Makes Angels Out Of
Men Who Sincerely Pursue It

      1. But mankind, inferior in its nature to blessed
spirits, strains beyond its capacity and, in so far as it
can, vies eagerly to equal the angels. How does it do
that? Angels neither marry nor are given in marriage;[34]
this is true of the virgin. The angels have stood continuously by God and serve him; so does the virgin. Accordingly, Paul has removed all cares from virgins "to
promote what is good, what will help you to devote yourselves entirely (to God)."[35] If they are unable for a
time to ascend to heaven as the angels can because their

flesh holds them back, even in this world they have much
consolation since they receive the Master of the heavens,
if they are holy in body and spirit.

2. Do you grasp the value of virginity? that it
makes those who spend time on earth live like the angels
dwelling in heaven? It does not allow those endowed with
bodies to be inferior to the incorporeal powers and spurs
all men to rival the angels. But this applies in no way
to you, who dishonor so great a virtue, who slander the
Lord and call him wicked. The punishment of painful
slavery will await you; but the virgins of the Church will
meet with many magnificent blessings that will surpass the
comprehension of the human eye, ear and thought. Therefore, dismissing the heretics—for enough has been said
about them—let us now speak to the children of the Church.

XII
When Paul Says: "As For The Other
Matters, I, Not The Lord, Say...,"
He Has Not Expressed Human Advice

1. Where would it be best to begin the discussion?
with the very words of the Lord, which are spoken by Saint
Paul. For we must believe his preaching is that of the
Lord. When he says: "To those now married I give this
command (though it is not mine; it is the Lord's),"[36] and
again: "As for the other matters, I, not the Lord, say
...,"[37] he does not mean that some words are his, and
others the Lord's. How could the man who has Christ
speaking in him, who is not anxious to live so that Christ
live in him,[38] who sets in second place after his love for
the Lord a kingdom, life, the angels and powers, and every
other creature, in short everything, how could he endure
either speaking or thinking anything that was not pleasing
to Christ, especially when he is laying down a precept?

2.   What, then, is his meaning when he says: "I,"
and "not I"? Christ has given us some laws and dogmas
himself and others through his apostles. He has not established them all himself. Hear what he says: "I have
much more to tell you, but you cannot bear it now."[39] So,
the law that "a woman not be separated from her husband,"
was promulgated first by Christ when he was physically on
the earth.[40] Because of this Paul says: "To those now
married I give this command (though it is not mine, but
the Lord's)." As for the unbelievers, the Lord says nothing himself to us, but inspiring the soul of Paul on this
point, he prescribed this law: "If any brother has a wife
who is an unbeliever but is willing to live with him, he
must not divorce her. And if any woman has a husband who
is an unbeliever but is willing to live with her, she must
not divorce him."[41]

3.   And so Paul said: "Not the Lord, but I," not because he wished to indicate that these words were of human
origin—how could they be?—but that the Lord had given
this command not when he was present with his disciples,
but now, through Paul. Accordingly, just as the phrase,
"The Lord, not I," does not contradict the command of
Christ, so the phrase, "I, not the Lord," is in no way a
personal expression contrary to God's will but an indication of this only, that his command is now being given
through his apostle.

4.   Indeed, when he discusses widowhood, the apostle
says: "She will be happier, though, in my opinion, if she
stays unmarried."[42] Then, so that you do not think it human reasoning when you hear "in my opinion," he has removed this suspicion by adding: "I am persuaded that in
this I have the Spirit of God." Therefore, just as when
he says that the words of the Spirit itself are his
opinion and we will not for this reason say the statement

is of human origin, so even at this point when he says:
"I am speaking, not the Lord," you should not think because of this that it is the word of Paul. For he has
Christ speaking in him, and he would not have dared to
frame so important a doctrine if he were not conveying the
law to us from him.

    5. Someone may respond: "As a believer I cannot en-
dure living with a woman who is not; I cannot live as a
pure man with an accursed wife. You yourself said earlier
that you say these things, not the Lord. Where is there
a guarantee for me?" But Paul would reply: "Do not be
afraid. I said that I have Christ speaking in me and that
'I am persuaded I have the Spirit of God' so that you suspect nothing human in what was said. If this were not so,
I would not attribute so much authority to my thoughts.
'For the deliberations of mortals are timid, and unsure
are our plans.'"[43] The universal Church also demonstrates
the strength of this law and watches over it scrupulously;
it would not do so if it had not been completely persuaded
that the words were a command of Christ.

    6. What, then, does Paul say under the inspiration
of the Lord? "Now for the matters you wrote about. A
man is better off having no relations with woman."[44] Here
one could congratulate the Corinthians for questioning
Paul before he brought the subject up, since they never
received any counsel from their master about virginity.
In this way, they indicated the progress they already
made thanks to grace. For from the time of the ancient
covenant there was no question about marriage. Not only
did all the people but even the Levites, the priests, and
the chief priest himself treated marriage with great respect.

XIII
Why The Corinthians Wrote To Paul About
Virginity And Why He Did Not Exhort
Them To Practice It Before This Time

1. How, then, did the Corinthians arrive at this
question? They quickly and quite rightly perceived that
they needed more virtue since they were deemed worthy of
a greater gift. It is appropriate to inquire why the
apostle had never instructed them in this, for, if they
had learned of any such counsel, they would not have written again asking the question anew. In fact, here we can
observe the depth of Paul's wisdom. He did not omit giving advice on so important a matter without a reason. Instead, he waited for them to first desire counsel and have
some perception of the nature of the problem, so that
finding their souls already receptive to the idea of virginity, he might profitably sow his words among them; for
the right attitude of one's listeners provides the appropriate frame of mind for receiving one's counsel. In addition, he underscores the loftiness and majesty of the
matter.

2. He would not have waited for an indication of
their readiness if it were not so; rather he would have
introduced the subject himself previously, if not as an
injunction or precept, at least as a recommendation and
counsel. By refusing to act first, he has clearly established that virginity requires much effort and a great
struggle. Even in this he has imitated our common Master,
for he too did not discuss virginity when his disciples
asked him.

3. When his disciples said: "If that is the case
between man and wife, it is better not to marry,"[45] Christ
replied: "There are some men who have castrated themselves
for the kingdom of heaven."[46] For when it is a matter of

a magnificent act of virtue (which is therefore not obligatory), it is necessary to wait for the willingness of
those intending to act rightly and in some other unsus-
pected way to instill in them the will and the desire,
just as Christ did. He did not implant a desire for virginity in their minds by talking about it. No, by discussing marriage alone and by pointing out its burdensome
character, and then saying no more, he managed the subject
wisely. The result was that his listeners, hearing nothing about not marrying, declared on their own: "It is
better not to marry."

    4. Accordingly, Paul, the imitator of Christ, said:
"Now for the matters you wrote about,"[47] not only to explain his silence but even to indicate this: I did not
dare lead you to this lofty peak because of the difficulty
of obtaining it. Since you have written me first, with
confidence I advise that a man is better off having no relations with a woman. Why did he nowhere add this counsel
when they wrote to him about many questions? For no
other reason than what I have just stated. He reminds
them of the letters they sent so that no one be annoyed
at his exhortation. Even so, he uses no strong language
in his exhortation but, taking advantage of the occasion,
he has employed instead much restraint, in this way too
imitating Christ. For the Savior, after completing his
talk on virginity added: "Let him accept this teaching
who can."[48] What then does Paul say? "Now for the matters you wrote about. A man is better off having no relations with a woman."

XIV.
Objection Of Those Who Reject
Virginity And Refutation

    1. Someone would object perhaps: if it is better to

have no relations with a woman, why has marriage been introduced into life? What use, then, will woman be to us,
if she is of help neither in marriage nor in the procreation of children? What will prevent the complete disap-
pearance of the human race since each day death encroaches
upon it and strikes man down, and if one follows this pro-
gramme, there is no reproduction of others to replace the
stricken? If all of us should strive after this virtue
and have no relations with a woman, everything—cities,
households, cultivated fields, crafts, animals, plants—
everything would vanish. For just as when a general dies,
the discipline of the army inevitably is thrown entirely
into confusion, so if the ruler of all on earth, if mankind disappears because of not marrying, nothing left
behind will preserve the security and good order of the
world, and this fine precept will fill the world with a
thousand woes.

     2. If these words had been merely those of our ene-
mies and the unbelievers, I would have hardly considered
them. However, many of those who appear to belong to the
Church say this. They fail to make an effort on behalf
of virginity because of their weakness of purpose. By
denigrating it and representing it as superfluous, they
want to conceal their own apathy, so that they seem to
fail in these contests not through their own neglect of
duty but rather through their correct estimation of the
matter. Come then, having dismissed our enemies—for
"The natural man does not accept what is taught by the
Spirit of God. For him, that is absurdity."[49]—let us
teach two lessons to those who claim to be with us: that
virginity is not superfluous but extremely useful and
necessary; and that such a charge is not made with impunity but will endanger the detractors in the same way
that right actions will earn wages and praise for the

virtuous.

3. When the whole world had been completed and all
had been readied for our repose and use, God fashioned
man for whom he made the world. After being fashioned,
man remained in paradise and there was no reason for marriage. Man did need a helper, and she came into being;
not even then did marriage seem necessary. It did not
yet appear anywhere but they remained as they were without
it. They lived in paradise as in heaven and they enjoyed
God's company. Desire for sexual intercourse, conception,
labor, childbirth and every form of corruption had been
banished from their souls. As a clear river shooting
forth from a pure source, so were they in that place
adorned by virginity.

4. And all the earth was without humanity. This
is what is now feared by those who are anxious about the
world. They are very anxious about the affairs of others
but they cannot tolerate considering their own. They fear
the eclipse of mankind but individually neglect their own
souls as though they were another's. They do this when
they will have demanded of them an exact accounting for
this and the smallest of sins, yet for the scarcity of
mankind they will not have to furnish even the slightest
excuse.

5. At that time there were no cities, crafts, or
houses—since you care so very much for these things—
they did not exist. Nevertheless, nothing either thwarted
or hindered that happy life, which was far better than
this. But when they did not obey God and became earth and
dust, they destroyed along with that blessed way of life
the beauty of virginity, which together with God abandoned
them and withdrew.[50] As long as they were uncorrupted by
the devil and stood in awe of their master, virginity

abided with them. It adorned them more than the diadem
and golden raiments do kings. However, when they shed
the princely raiment of virginity and laid aside their
heavenly attire, they accepted the decay of death, ruin,
pain, and a toilsome life. In their wake came marriage:
marriage, a garment befitting mortals and slaves.

6. "But the married man is busy with this world's
demands."[51] Do you perceive the origin of marriage? why
it seems to be necessary? It springs from disobedience,
from a curse, from death. For where death is, there is
marriage. When one does not exist, the other is not about.
But virginity does not have this companion. It is always
useful, always beautiful and blessed, both before and
after death, before and after marriage. Tell me, what
sort of marriage produced Adam? What kind of birth pains
produced Eve? You could not say. Therefore why have
groundless fears? Why tremble at the thought of the end
of marriage, and thus the end of the human race? An in-
finite number of angels are at the service of God, thousands upon thousands of archangels are beside him, and
none of them have come into being from the succession of
generations, none from childbirth, labor pains and conception. Could he not, then, have created many more men without marriage? Just as he created the first two from whom
all men descend.

XV
Marriage Does Not Increase
The Human Race

1. And today our race is not increased by the authority of marriage but by the word of our Lord, who said
at the beginning: "Be fertile and multiply; fill the
earth."[52] How did marriage help Abraham in the procreation of children? After participating in it for so many

years, did he not finally cry out: "Master, what will you
give me? Am I to die childless?"[53] Even as God at that
time had provided from lifeless bodies the foundation and
roots for so many thousands of descendants, so at the beginning too, if those about Adam had obeyed his commands
and overcome their desire for the forbidden tree, they
would not have needed a means of increasing the race of
men. For marriage will not be able to produce many men if
God is unwilling, nor will virginity destroy their number
if he wishes there to be many of them. But he wanted it
to be so, Scripture says, because of us and our disobedience.

2. Why did marriage not appear before the treachery? Why was there no intercourse in paradise? Why not
the pains of childbirth before the curse? Because at that
time these things were superfluous. The necessity arose
later because of our weakness, as did cities, crafts, the
wearing of clothes, and all our other numerous needs.
Death introduced them in its wake. Moreover, do not prefer this, a concession to your own weakness, to virginity;
or rather, do not assign marriage to an equal rank. If
you follow this reasoning, you will say it is better to
have two wives instead of being content with only one
since this had been allowed under the law of Moses. In
the same way, you will also prefer wealth to voluntary
poverty, luxury to a moderate way of life, and revenge to
a noble endurance of injustice.

XVI
Marriage Is A Concession To Us

1. Someone objects: You are denigrating these ancient laws. Not at all, for God has permitted them, and
they were useful in their time. Yet, I say that they are
of little value and are the virtues of children, not men.

For this reason, Christ, desiring to make us perfect, has
ordered us to lay them aside as though they were children's garments that cannot encompass the complete man
nor adorn that perfect man who is Christ come to full
stature.[54] He asks us to put on clothes more fitting and
perfect than these. He has not contradicted himself.
Indeed he is very consistent.

    2. Although the new commandments are superior to
the old, the aim of the lawgiver is the same. What is it?
To reduce the baseness of our soul and to lead it to perfect virtue. Therefore, if God had been anxious not to
dictate obligations greater than the former ones but to
leave things eternally the same and never to release men
from that inferior state, he completely contradicted himself. If at the beginning, in fact, when the human race
was more childlike, God had prescribed this regimented
way of life, we would never have accepted it with moderation but would have completely jeopardized our salvation
through immoderation. Similarly, if after a long period
of training under the old law when the time called us to
this heavenly philosophy, if then he had permitted us to
remain on earth, we would have gained nothing much from
his concession since we had no part in that perfection
on account of which his indulgence arose.

XVII
About God's Concession
To Human Limitations

    1. Our situation today resembles that of nest-
lings: after the mother has reared them, she escorts
them from the nest. If she sees they are weak and stumble, still in need of a haven within, she permits them
to stay longer, not so that they remain within the nest
forever, but so that when their wings have become very

strong and all their strength has been gathered together,
they can fly off with security. In the same way, the
Lord drew us from the beginning toward heaven and pointed
out the road leading there. He did so with the sure
knowledge, no doubt, that we would not be strong enough
for that flight. He wanted to show us that our fall was
not his intention but the result of our own weakness.
After he has shown this, he allows us from then on to be
reared in the world and in marriage, even as in the nest,
for a long time.

    2. Since our wings of virtue grew over a long pe-
riod of time, gently at first, little by little, he came
and led us here away from the nest and taught us how to
fly higher. Those who are more plodding in nature and
are in a deep sleep still haunt the nest and are attached
to worldly things. The truly noble, the lovers of light,
however, quit the nest with great ease and fly high in
the air and skim the heavens. Everything is left behind
on earth: marriage, money, cares and all else that customarily drags us down to earth.

    3. Let us not think, therefore, that the power to
marry, which arose in the beginning, is binding upon us
for the future and keeps us from withdrawing from marriage. God wants us to leave it behind. Hear his words:
"Let him accept this teaching who can."[55] Do not be surprised that he had not ordered this at the beginning. A
doctor for example does not prescribe everything all at
once to his patients. When they are seized by a fever,
he keeps them from solid food; but when the fever and
accompanying physical weakness subside, he bans disagreeable foods from that point on and returns the patients
to their customary regime. In the body, when the elemen-
tary principles quarrel with each other, they cause illness by their excesses or deficiencies; in the soul, the

unruliness of the emotions ruins its health. It is also necessary above all else to have at the right moment the appropriate precept for the emotions in question, since without both of these conditions the law by itself would be powerless to correct the disorder in the soul. Just as the essence of drugs could not by itself heal a wound, the same is true of laws in general: for what drugs are to injuries, laws are to sins.

4. You do not meddle with the physician when he lances a wound or when he cauterizes it or when he does neither. Yet he often fails. Do you, a man, interfere with God who never fails, who manages everything in a manner worthy of his wisdom? Will you demand of him an accounting of his commandments? Will you not defer to his boundless wisdom? Is this not the height of madness? He said: "Be fertile and multiply," which the times required since man's nature raved and was unable to contain its violent passions and had no other haven amid that storm.

5. But what commandment was necessary? To live in continence and virginity? That would have produced a more disastrous result and a more violent fire of passion. Indeed, if children who need only milk were removed from the nurture proper for man and were forced to alter their diet, nothing would keep them from dying at once; so grievous is the untimeliness of that action. For this reason, virginity was not granted from the beginning. No, rather, virginity did appear at the beginning and was prior to marriage. Marriage was introduced later for the reasons cited and was thought necessary. Adam would not have needed it if he had remained obedient. You will ask if all men were to be created in this manner. Yes, either in this way or in another that I cannot say. The point is that God did not need marriage for the creation

of a multitude of men upon the earth.

XVIII
It Is Not Virginity That
Decreases The Race Of Men But Sin

Virginity does not cause the human race to dry up
but sin and unnatural intercourse do, which was proven
in Noah's time when men, their flocks, and everything
else living on earth was destroyed.[56] If the sons of
God had checked that unnatural desire then and esteemed
virginity, if they had not seen the daughters of men with
wicked eyes,[57] so disastrous an end would not have overtaken them. Let no one think that I blame marriage for
their destruction, for I do not say that; but I do say
the ruin and destruction of our species results not
from virginity but from sin.

XIX
There Were Formerly Two
Reasons For Marriage But Now One

1. So marriage was granted for the sake of procreation, but an even greater reason was to quench the
fiery passion of our nature. Paul attests to this when
he says: "But to avoid immorality, every man should have
his own wife."[58] He does not say: for the sake of procreation. Again, he asks us to engage in marriage not
to father many children, but why? so "that Satan may not
tempt you," he says.[59] Later he does not say: if they
desire children but "if they cannot exercise self-control,
they should marry." At the beginning, as I said, marriage had these two purposes but now, after the earth and
sea and all the world has been inhabited, only one reason
remains for it: the suppression of licentiousness and debauchery.

2. Marriage is of much use to those who are still
now caught up in their passions, who desire to live the
life of swine and be ruined in brothels. It rescues them
from that impure compulsion and keeps them holy and
chaste. But when will I stop this useless arguing? You
who object know as well as we do the superiority of virginity. All your words are excuses, pretexts, and ruses
for your incontinence.

XX

If There Is No Danger For Those
Who Despise Virginity, That Does
Not Mean No Risks Are Involved

If it were possible to make such remarks without
danger, it would be necessary, nevertheless, to now end
the slander. For when a man is faced with the good but
inclines toward the opposite, in addition to harming himself in other ways, he offers to the world no small proof
of his own depravity, namely, a judgment perverted and
wicked. If, then, for no other reason than for the sake
of not acquiring a bad reputation it were necessary to
hold your tongue, consider this well: when a spectator
admires the contestants who are conspicuous in the struggle, even if he could not attain their level, he would be
able at least to gain everyone's sympathy; but the man
who in addition to not participating also denigrates the
accomplishments that are worthy of many crowns, he would
rightly be hated by everyone for his aversion and hostility toward excellence. He would also be more wretched
than the insane, for the demented do not know what they
do and endure their lot unwillingly. Thus, when they
commit outrages against those in power, they go unpunished and are even treated with mercy by those they insulted. But if someone should voluntarily dare what

madmen do involuntarily, he would justifiably be condemned in everyone's judgment as an enemy of human nature.

XXI
The Detractors Of Virginity
Are In Great Peril

1. Thus, it would be necessary, as I said, to refrain from making such an accusation at least for the
reason stated, even if it involved no risks. But the
danger from such calumny is great. Not only will you
who "sit speaking against your brother; [who] against
your mother's son spread rumors"[60] be punished for the
offence, but he who tries to discredit things deemed
beautiful by God will also be punished. Hear at any rate
what another prophet says in his discussion about the
same topic: "Woe to those who call evil good, and good
evil, who change darkness into light, and light into
darkness, who change bitter into sweet, and sweet into
bitter!"[61] What is sweeter, more beautiful, more brilliant than virginity? Indeed, it sparkles more radiantly
than the very rays of the sun. It removes us from all
worldly affairs while preparing us to look with pure eyes
directly into the sun of justice. And Isaiah shouted
this out about those with perverted judgments.

2. Hear, too, what another prophet says about
those who proclaim these pestilent words to others. He
begins with the same expression: "Woe to you who give your
neighbors a flood of your wrath to drink."[62] The words
"Woe to" are not simply an expression but a threat fore-
telling unspeakable and merciless retribution. This in-
terjection in the Scriptures applies to those no longer
able to escape the imminent punishment.

3. And again another prophet accuses the Jews with
these words: "You gave the Nazirites wine to drink."[63]

If giving wine to the Nazirites brings about such severe
punishment, what punishment will he deserve who pours
out a flood of wrath to the souls of simpler people? If
someone is inevitably punished for not observing a small
part of the ascetic code, what penalty will he receive
who disparages sanctity altogether? "It would be better
for anyone who leads astray one of these little ones...
to be drown by a millstone around his neck, in the
depths of the sea."[64] How will they reply, then, who
tempt not one child but many to sin with these words?
If he who calls his brother a fool[65] will be led away directly to the fire of hell, how much anger will he call
down upon his head who attacks this angelic way of life?

   4. Once Miriam spoke against Moses,[66] not in the
manner in which you now do virginity, but to a lesser degree and with great moderation. She did not ridicule the
man nor scoff at the virtue of that blessed one; on
the contrary, she admired him very much. She only said
that she too enjoyed the same privileges that he did.
Nevertheless, she called down upon herself the wrath of
God. In spite of the passionate pleas of Moses, who ap-
peared to be the insulted party, her punishment was increased more than he expected.

                           XXII
              It Was Useful That The Children
              Perished In The Time Of Elisha

   1. Why do I speak of Miriam? The children who
played near the gates of Bethlehem to say to Elisha only
this: "Go up, bald head," so provoked God that at the
very moment of their taunt he let loose bears (forty-two
of them) upon their number. They were all completely
torn to pieces by those beasts.[67] Neither their age,

nor number, nor saying they were joking protected those
young boys, and rightly so. For if those who undertake great
tasks are disparaged by men and boys, what weaker souls
will choose to attempt deeds that are the subject of
laughter and mockery? Who from the multitude of men will
emulate virtuous action when he sees it is so ridiculed?

  2. Today, when virginity is admired everywhere by
all (not only by those who practice it but even by those
who have fallen from it), nevertheless if many people recoil from it and shirk those efforts, who would readily
wish to undertake it if, in addition to not being admired,
a general disparagement of it were discernible? The exceedingly strong in character, who have already departed
to heaven, have no need of exhortations from the multitude; approval from God is sufficient encouragement for
them. However, those weaker in nature, who are being led
by the hand to virginity derive much support from public
opinion, influential as it is, until after receiving instruction from all quarters they gradually no longer have
need of it.

  3. This came about not just because of the weak,
but also for the sake of the salvation of those who scoff
at virginity: they can now advance no further than that
evil with the thought they will go unpunished since they
did not pay a penalty for their former faults.

  In thinking about this, I recall the story of Elijah.
What the children suffered from the bears because of Elisha,
two groups of fifty men along with their captains suffered
from a fire kindled from above because of his teacher. For
when they visited Elijah and with great irony called him
the just and ordered him to come down to them, in his
place fire descended, which consumed them all just as the
wild beasts had the boys.[68]

  4. Therefore, take this into consideration all you

enemies of virginity and seal your lips at last, so that
you do not begin to say on the day of judgment when you
behold there those radiant with virginity: "Those are the
people whom we once thought laughable and objects of reproach. We foolishly regarded their way of life as madness and insulted their accomplishment. How have they
been counted among the sons of God? How is their lot with
the saints? We, then, have strayed from the way of truth
and the light of justice did not shine for us."[69]   But
what good will these words be when their repentance under
such circumstances loses its value?

XXIII
Why Those Who Commit The Same Sins
Are Not Punished In The Same Way

But perhaps one of you will say: Then, did no one
insult holy men after that? Many people have in many
places. Why, then, did they not receive the same punishment? They did and we know of many of them. If some of
them have escaped temporarily, they will not escape in
the end. According to Saint Paul: "Some men's sins are
flagrant and cry out for judgment now, while other men's
sins will appear only later."[70]   Even as legislators have
overlooked punishments for the guilty though they be established by law, so too our Lord Jesus Christ by punishing one or two sinners sets down like an inscription on a
bronze stele their punishment and uses their experiences
as a warning to all. It says that even if those who dare
the same sins do not suffer a similar penalty now, they
will suffer a harsher one in the future.

XXIV
Sinners Who Are Unpunished Should
Not Feel Confident But Rather
Fear More Because Of This

1. And so, when we go unpunished although we have
sinned grievously, let us not be confident but be more
fearful because of this. For if we are not judged here by
God, we will be condemned there with the world. Again,
this is not my pronouncement but that of Christ speaking
through Paul. Addressing those who take part in the sa-
craments without being worthy, he says: "That is why many
among you are sick and infirm, and why so many are dying.
If we were to examine ourselves, we would not be falling
under judgment in this way: but since it is the Lord who
judges us, he chastens us to keep us from being condemned
with the rest of the world."[71] There are those who need
criticism only here. Their sins are moderate in nature
and they no longer race back to their earlier errors like
a dog that returns to his vomit.[72] Yet there are those
who pay the penalty for their excessive wickedness both
here and there. Others are punished only in the next
world because they committed more serious sins than everyone else and are unworthy of being whipped with men. "And
they will not be scourged with men," Scripture says, since
they are being kept for punishment with the devils.[73]
"Out of my sight," it says, "into that darkness without
prepared for the devil and his angels."[74]

2. Many have stolen the priesthood with money without being censored for it and have not heard what Simon then
heard from Peter.[75] They have not escaped, however, but
will undergo a far harsher punishment than what is exacted
here because they were not chastened by the example. Many
ventured what Korah did but did not suffer his fate, but
they will later endure a greater punishment.[76] Many who

imitated the impiety of the Pharaoh were not drowned in
the sea as he was, but the sea of hell awaits them.[77]   Nor
have those who call their brothers fools paid the penalty:
their punishment has been reserved for them in hell.[78]

3. Moreover, do not think the judgments of God are
mere words. This is why he fulfilled some of them beforehand, as in the case of Sapphira and her husband,[79] of
Charmi,[80] of Aaron,[81] and of many others. God intended by
these examples that those who distrust his words and have
been troubled by actual occurrences stop deluding themselves from now on that they will not be punished, and
that they learn that the kindness of God consists of granting a respite to sinners, and not in not punishing at all
those who continue in their errors.

4. I could say more and point out how much fire
those who disparage the beauty of virginity bring down upon themselves, but this account suffices for sensible men.
It will not be possible to recall the incorrigible and the
insane from their madness with many more words than these.
Therefore, passing over this part of our discussion, let
us turn our attention entirely to sensible men and return
once again to Saint Paul. "Now for the matters you wrote
about," he says, "a man is better off having no relations
with a woman."[82] Let both those who denigrate marriage
and those who exalt it unduly now feel ashamed, for Paul
curbs both of them with these words and those that follow.

XXV
Marriage Is A Necessity For The Weak

Marriage is good because it keeps man chaste and does not
allow him to die engulfed by fornication. Therefore, do
not belittle it, for it has a great advantage in not letting the limbs of Christ become the limbs of a prostitute

and in not allowing his holy temple to become impure and
unclean.[83]   Thus, marriage is good because it supports
and sets right one about to falter.   But what has it to do
with someone who is erect and not in need of assistance
from it?   Then marriage is no longer useful or necessary
but an impediment to virtue, not only because it creates
many difficulties, but also because it deprives one of a
larger share of praise.

XXVI
The Man Who Is Capable Of Virginity
But Marries Hurts Himself The Most

The contestant who is completely armed with weapons
but who can fight and win when naked has not helped himself. He causes himself the worst injury by depriving
himself of admiration and gleaming crowns. He has not allowed all of his strength to shine or let his trophy be
much celebrated. In the case of marriage, the loss is
greater; for you deprive yourself of both the honor many
pay you and the wages in store for virginity. And so, "A
man is better off having no relations with a woman." Why
does Paul agree to relations with her? "But to avoid immorality, every man should have his own wife."[84] I am
afraid, Paul says, to lead you up to the heights of virginity in case you fall into the pit of fornication. Your
wings are not yet nimble enough for me to lift you to
that peak.——And yet they have chosen the rigors of the
contest and have leapt toward the beauty of virginity.
Why, then, are you afraid, why tremble, Saint Paul?——
Perhaps he would answer: because they are eager but still
ignorant about virginity; the experience and involvement
I have already had in this battle make me more hesitant
to recommend it to others.

XXVII
Virginity Is An Important Virtue
And The Source Of Great Benefits

1. I know the violence attendant upon this state.
I know the strain of these deeds. I know the burden of
the fight. You need a soul fond of strife, one forceful
and reckless against the passions. You must walk over
coals without being burned,[85] and walk over swords without
being slashed. The power of passion is as great as that
of fire and sword. If the soul happens not to have been
prepared in this way to be indifferent to its suffering,
it will quickly destroy itself. We need iron will, eyes
always open, much patience, strong defences, external walls
and barriers, watchful and high-minded guards, and in addition to all of these, divine help. For "unless the Lord
guard the city, in vain does the guard keep vigil."[86]
        2. How will we obtain this help? By giving all of
ourselves: by reasoning soundly, by enduring the strain of
fasting and sleeplessness, by adhering strictly to the
rules of conduct and observing the precepts, and above all,
by not being overconfident in ourselves. If we happen to
have been very successful, we must say to ourselves constantly: "Unless the Lord build the house, they labor in
vain who build it."[87] For "our battle is not against human forces but against the principalities and the power,
the rulers of this world of darkness, the evil spirits in
regions above."[88] Day and night we must stand armed with
arguments and appear formidable to these shameful passions.
When they arouse us just a little, the devil stands by
with fire in hand ready to burn down the temple of God.
Therefore, we must be fortified on all sides. Our battle
is against natural compulsions. We emulate the life of
the angels. Our race is with the incorporeal powers.
Earth and dust compete eagerly to equal the life of those

in heaven, and corruption has undertaken battle with in-
corruption.[89]

    3. Tell me, who will still dare to compare the
pleasure of marriage with so magnificent a state? Is it
not too simple-minded? Aware of all this, Paul said:
"Every man should have his own wife." This is why he
hesitated, this is why he feared discussing virginity with
them from the start. He continued to speak about marriage
with the desire of turning them gradually away from it,
then keeping his discussion of continence brief, he inter-
spersed in it many words on marriage, thereby not allowing
them to be struck by the harshness of his exhortations.
When a speaker from beginning to end interweaves his
speech with rather harsh advice, he is tiresome to his
audience and often forces the soul to recoil because it
cannot tolerate the weight of his words. However, when
the speaker embroiders his talk and arranges a mixture of
topics in which the most agreeable outweighs the disagreeable, he disguises the weightiness of the matter. By allowing the listener to rest, he thus persuades and influences him more, as even Saint Paul did.

    4. For after he says: "A man is better off having
no relations with a woman,"[90] he straightway takes up marriage and says: "Every man should have his own wife."[91]
While he pronounces virginity alone blessed, he passes
over it with the words: "A man is better off having no relations with a woman." But with respect to marriage, he
advises and orders it, and he adds his reason: "To avoid
immorality." Thus he seems to account for his acquiescence to marriage. In fact, although the audience is un-
aware of it, he praises continence while giving pretexts
for marriage. He does not reveal this thought clearly in
his speech but leaves it behind in the consciousness of

his listeners. For the man who learns that marriage is
advised not because it is the height of virtue but because
Paul has condemned him for having so much lust that without marriage he is incapable of restraining it, this man
blushing with shame will hastily pursue virginity and be
anxious to divest himself of such ill repute.

XXVIII
Paul's Words About Marriage Are
An Exhortation To Virginity

1. What does he say next? "The husband should fulfill his conjugal obligations toward his wife, the wife
hers toward her husband."[92] Then, to explain and clarify
this, he adds: "A wife does not belong to herself but to
her husband; a husband does not belong to himself but to
his wife."[93] This seems to be said in defense of marriage;
but, in fact, he is wrapping the hook with familiar bait,
and coaxing his disciples to his way of thinking. He desires by these very words about marriage to lead them
from it. For when you hear that you will not be your own
master after marriage but be subject to the will of your
wife, you will quickly aspire not to pass under the yoke
at all, since once you have entered into this state, you
must be a slave henceforth, so long as it pleases your wife.

2. It is easy to learn from the disciples that I am
not simply conjecturing about Paul's opinion. They did
not think at first that marriage was burdensome or oppres-
sive until they heard the Lord forcing them to the conclusion that the Corinthians were led to by Paul. The
statements: "Everyone who divorces his wife—lewd conduct
is a separate case—forces her to commit adultery,"[94] and
"a husband does not belong to himself" express the same
idea in different words.

3. To consider Paul's words more carefully, he in-

creases the tyranny of marriage and makes the servitude
appear more burdensome. For the Lord did not permit a
husband to drive his wife from the house, whereas Paul
takes away a man's authority over his own body and sur-
renders dominion over it to his wife; and he ranks a
husband lower than a slave bought with silver. It is
often possible for a slave to obtain absolute freedom if
he can gain at some time enough money to pay his price
to his master. But even if a husband had the most troublesome wife of all, he must bear with his servitude, and
he can discover no deliverance or way out of this despo-
tism.

XXIX
The Command: "Do Not Deprive One Another "
Is An Exhortation To Virginity

1. After stating: "A wife does not belong to herself," Paul adds: "Do not deprive one another, unless
perhaps by mutual consent for a time, to devote yourselves to prayer and fasting. Then return to one another."[95] I think that many of those who have embarked
upon virginity blush and are ashamed at this point by
Paul's great concession. Do not be afraid, and do not
be foolish. These words seem to be favorable to those
who have married, but if you examine them closely you
will find they are similar in thought to his earlier
words. If you should simply desire to attack this reasoning by removing it from its context, the word will appear spoken by a bridesmaid, not an apostle. But if you
should follow the point of his discussion, you will discover this timely counsel to be worthy of the apostle.

Why, in fact, does Paul treat this subject at
greater length? Was it not sufficient for him to solemn-
ly indicate by his earlier remarks his thoughts and to

end his advice there? How are these two statements: "The
husband should fulfill his conjugal obligations toward
his wife," and "a husband does not belong to himself,"
amplified by "Do not deprive one another, unless perhaps
by mutual consent for a time?"[96] Not at all, but by this
addition Paul has clarified what was stated there briefly
and obscurely.

2. In this he imitates the holy man of God, Samuel,
who interprets with great precision the laws of the mon-
archy for private citizens not with the intention of
having them accepted, but the very opposite. Although
Samuel seems to be instructing them, in fact he is de-
flecting their ill-timed desire. It is the same with
Paul, only he more constantly and clearly reflects upon
the tyranny of marriage in his desire to rescue them
from it with his words. He says: "A wife does not belong
to herself," but he adds: "Do not deprive one another,
unless perhaps by mutual consent, to devote yourselves
to prayer and fasting." Do you see how he has led married people unsuspecting and without offence to the exercise of continence? Initially he simply commended it,
saying: "A man is better off having no relations with a
woman." He adds at this point his recommendation when he
says: "Do not deprive one another, unless by mutual consent."

3. Why has he not simply commanded what he wants
instead of expressing it as a recommendation? For he
has not said: Deprive one another but do so by mutual
consent, so that you have time for prayer, but "Do not
deprive one another, unless by mutual consent." He does
so because this manner of expression is milder. It il-
luminates the teacher's sentiment by not rigidly requir-
ing this conduct, which is accomplished above all amid

much generosity. Thus, he encourages his listener and
reduces the harsh aspects of his speech to brief remarks.
Before his listener becomes distressed, he returns to the
more agreeable subject and dwells upon it further.

XXX
If Marriage Is Honored, Why
Does The Apostle Recommend
Continence To Those Who Fast?

1. It is worthwhile to examine this point too: if
indeed marriage is honored and the marriage-bed undefiled,[97] why does Paul not permit intercourse during the
time of fasting and prayer? Because it would be very
strange that the Jews—for whom all bodily needs had been
regulated, who were allowed to have two wives and then to
reject them and introduce others in their place—had so
much foresight that they abstained from even legitimate
intercourse when they were about to hear divine words, and
did so not for one or two days, but for several, but that
we who enjoy so much grace, who have received the Spirit,
who when dead are buried with Christ, who have been deemed
worthy of being adopted as his sons, who have been raised
to such an honor, that we after so many great favors have
not acquired the same zeal as those little children.

2. If someone should continue to question why Moses
himself directed the Jews away from intercourse, I would
reply that even if marriage is esteemed, it could only be
beneficial in so far as it does not corrupt the one who
contracts it. It has not the power to make saints, but
virginity does. Moses and Paul are not alone in requesting it. Hear what Joel says: "Proclaim a fast, call
an assembly,...assemble the elders."[98] Perhaps you look
to see where he has bid them to withdraw from women. "Let

the bridegroom quit his room, and the bride her chamber."
Indeed this command is more comprehensive than that of
Moses. For if the bridegroom and bride, in whom carnal
desire is at its peak, who burst with youth and whose desire is ungovernable, if they must not have intercourse
during the period of fasting and prayer, under how much
more obligation are other men who lack this tremendous
urge for sex? He who prays and fasts as he ought must
renounce every human desire, every care, every kind of
wasteful occupation, and in this way with perfect concen-
tration approach God. This is why fasting is a fine act:
it trims cares away from the soul, and by keeping neglect
of duty from overrunning the mind turns the intellect entirely towards itself. Paul implies this when he diverts
us from sexual intercourse. His words are extremely apt.
He does not say: so that you not be defiled, but: "to devote yourselves to prayer and fasting," as if intercourse
with a woman does not lead to impurity but to a waste of
time.

XXXI
Paul Had To Divert From Coitus Those
Intending To Devote Their Time To Prayer

Since today amid so much security the devil tries
to thwart us during prayer, if he comes upon a soul dissipated and softened by an attachment to a woman, what
effect will he produce by diverting the eyes of our mind
this way and that? To avoid this eventuality and to keep
us from offending God with so profane a prayer at the
very moment we are especially eager to render him favor-
ably disposed to us, Paul bids us to abstain from coitus
at that time.

XXXII
By Praying Indifferently Not Only Do We
Not Appease God, We Even Provoke Him

1. Those who appear before kings—but why do I say
kings?—when slaves make their petition before the lowest
magistrates and lords, whether they do so because they
have suffered injustices from others or to ask for favors
for themselves, or because they are anxious to dispel any
anger directed at themselves, they turn their eyes and
complete attention to their superiors, and in this way
make their petition. If they have neglected the smallest
detail, they are not only unsuccessful in their request,
they are even pushed away and ill-treated to boot. If
those who desire to appease human anger have to take such
great pains, what will become of us, poor creatures that
we are, who approach God, the master of all, with so much
indifference, when we are the object of a much greater
anger for doing so? For no servant would provoke a master
or subject a king as we do God each day.

2. Christ makes this point when he assesses sins
against one's neighbor in denarii but counts those against
God as equal to a thousand talents.[99] Therefore, when we
approach him in prayers to quiet his great wrath and to
reconcile ourselves with him whom we have irritated each
day, Paul naturally leads us from these sexual pleasures
all but saying: it is a question of our souls, beloved,
we are in great jeopardy; we must tremble, we must be
fearful, we must cower together. We approach an awesome
master who has been much offended by us, a master who
considers us to be very blameworthy and censures us for
grievous faults. This is not the time for embraces or
pleasures, but for tears and bitter moaning, supplication,
scrupulous confession, earnest petition and much prayer.
We must be content if by approaching him with so much

zeal we can appease his anger—not that our master is
harsh or cruel, in fact he is very gentle and benevolent.
But the excessiveness of our sins does not allow him to
quickly pardon us although he is good-natured, kind and
very merciful.

3.   Therefore Paul says: "to devote yourselves to
prayer and fasting." What, then, could be more bitter
than this bondage? Do you wish, he says to advance toward virtue, to fly up to heaven, to wipe clean the stain
from your soul through constant fasting and prayer? If
your wife does not wish to agree to this, you must be
subject to her lust. This is why he said at the beginning: "A man is better off having no relations with a woman." Therefore the disciples said to the Lord: "If that
is the case between man and wife, it is better not to
marry."[100] Reasoning that there had to be in each case
disadvantages, they were forced upon reflection to make
this statement.

                              XXXIII
                  To Repeat, To Practice Virginity
                       Is To Imitate Christ

        Thus Paul continually returns to this point in
order to lead the Corinthians to this reasoning: "Every
man should have his own wife; the husband should fulfill
his conjugal obligations toward his wife; a wife does not
belong to herself; do not deprive one another; return to
one another."[101] For the blessed apostles did not grasp
at once Christ's meaning from his first words on the subject, but when they heard it repeated, then they were
aware of the imperative nature of his remarks. When
Christ was sitting on the mountain, he discussed continence and returned to it again after treating many
other subjects. In this way he led them to the love of

it.[102]   Thus do statements that are constantly repeated
have greater force. Here, then, the apostle Paul, imitating the Master, discusses his topic continuously. Nowhere does he simply set forth his consent for marriage,
but rather he always adds the reason: "Because of fornication, the temptations of Satan and incontinence." And
so, he subtly praises virginity when he speaks about
marriage.

XXXIV
Virginity Is Admirable
And Worthy Of Many Crowns

1.   If Paul has feared separating for a long period
those who live in the state of marriage out of his concern that the devil may discover a way to their souls,
how many crowns would those women deserve who needed no
such encouragement to begin with and who persevere to the
end unconquered? Yet the cunning work of the devil is
not applied in the same way to each case. I think he
does not harass the former group because he knows that
they have a place of refuge close by. If they experience
too violent an attack, it is possible to flee directly to
that haven. Saint Paul does not allow them to sail out
too far but advises them to turn round whenever they tire
and to renew the communal life. The virgin, on the other
hand, is of necessity entirely at sea and sails a harbor-
less ocean. If a very severe storm arises, it is not her
right to anchor ship and rest.

2.   Therefore it is like pirates on the sea: they
do not attack ships where there is a city, seaport or
harbor, for this involves a useless risk. But if they
intercept a ship on the high sea, since they have solitude
for their work with no chance of someone coming to the
rescue, this situation feeds their recklessness. They

ransack and overturn everything, and do not stop until
they have drown the crew or suffered this fate themselves.
This is how that dread pirate assaults the virgin: with a
great storm accompanied by a distressful surging of the
sea and towering waves. Tossing her this way and that he
so confounds everything that he overturns her ship with
brute force. He has heard that the virgin has no recourse
to the married state of intimacy but must wrestle entirely
by herself and battle against the spirits of evil until
she puts into a truly calm harbor.

3. Paul shuts the virgin outside the walls like a
brave soldier and he does not permit opening the gates to
her, even if the enemy rages against her, even if the enemy becomes more violent precisely because his adversary
has no means of ending the action. The devil is not alone
in harassing the unmarried. The sting of desire does this,
too, with greater urgency. This is clear to all, for we
are not quickly overcome by the desire for things that we
enjoy, since the licence to enjoy them allows the soul to
be indifferent to them. A proverb, popular and quite true,
attests to this: what is within our grasp does not excite
strong desire. However, once forbidden what we were formerly masters of, the opposite results, and what was
scorned by us when we had authority over it arouses in us
a more violent desire whenever we lose this power.

4. This is the first reason why there is more se-
renity among married people. The second is that even if
at times the flame of passion struggles in them to reach
a climax, sexual intercourse follows and swiftly represses
it. But the virgin on the other hand has no remedy to ex-
tinguish the fire. She sees it rising to a crescendo and
coming to a peak, but she lacks the power to put it out.
Her only chance is to fight the fire so that she is not

burnt. Is there, then, anything more extraordinary than
carrying within one all of this fire and not being burnt?
To collect in the inner chambers of the soul this fire but
to keep one's thoughts untouched by it? No one concedes
to the virgin the right of emptying these coals of passion
outside herself, yet what the author of Proverbs says is
impossible for our bodies, she is compelled to endure in
her soul. What does he say? "Will someone walk upon
burning coal and not burn his feet?"[103] But behold, she
walks upon it and bears the torture! "Will someone wrap
fire in the fold of his garments without his clothes burning?" The virgin has the provocative fire roaring not
within her clothes, but within herself, yet she sustains
and endures the flame.

5. Tell me, will someone still dare to compare marriage with virginity? Or look marriage in the face at all?
Saint Paul does not permit it. He puts much distance between each of these states. "The virgin is concerned with
things of the Lord," he says, but "the married woman has
the cares of this world to absorb her."[104] Moreover,
after gathering married people together and having done
this favor for them, hear how he reproaches them again for
he says: "Return to one another, that Satan may not tempt
you."[105] And since he wishes to indicate that not all sins
stem from the devil's temptations but from our own idleness,
he has added the more valid reason: because of "your lack
of self-control."[106]

6. Who would not blush hearing this? Who would not
earnestly try to escape blame for incontinence? For this
exhortation is not for everyone but for those extremely
prone to vice. If you are enslaved by pleasures, he says,
if you are so weak as to have always given way to coitus
and to gape in eager expectation at it, be joined to a
woman. The consent therefore comes not from one approving

or praising this action but from one scoffing at it with
derision. If it had not been his desire to assail the
souls of pleasure-seekers, he would not have set down this
term "incontinence," which quite emphatically conveys the
idea of censure. Why did he not say "because of your weakness?" Because that phrase is one of indulgence but to say
incontinence denotes excessive moral laxity. Thus, the
inability to refrain from fornication unless you always
have a wife and enjoy sexual relations is an indication of
incontinence.

7. What would those people who consider virginity
superfluous say at this point? For the more virginity is
practiced the more praise it receives, whereas marriage is
deprived of all praise especially when someone has used it
immoderately. "I say this," Paul declares, "by way of concession, not as a command."[107] But where there is a concession there is no place for praise. He also said, however, in his discussion of virgins: "I have not received
any commandment from the Lord, but I give my opinion."[108]
Has he not undercut his own position? Not at all. In the
case of virginity he has given his opinion but in the case
of marriage he makes a concession. He orders neither the
one nor the other but not for the same reason: in the one
case, so that anyone who desires to rise above incontinence
not be restrained, as he would be if bound by an injunction;
but in the other case, so that someone incapable of ascend-
ing to virginity not be condemned for having disobeyed a
commandment. I do not order you to live as virgins, he
says; for I fear the difficulty of the task. I do not order you to continually have relations with your wife; for
I do not wish to be the legislator of incontinence. I
have said "return to one another" with the intention of
keeping you from sinking lower, not to check your willingness to advance higher.

8. You see, it is not his intention to lead you to
continually resorting to your wife, but the incontinence
of those weaker morally requires this rule. If you wish to
learn the will of Paul, hear what it is: "I should like you
to be as I am,"[109] that is, continent.—So, if you want all
men to be continent, you want no one to marry.—No, not at
all. I do not prevent those who want to marry, nor do I
reproach them, but I pray and long for all men to be as I
myself am. However, I give my consent to marriage because
of fornication. Therefore, I said at the beginning: "A
man is better off having no relations with a woman."

XXXV
Paul Presented Himself As An Example
Continence Out Of Necessity

1. Why does Paul at this point mention himself with
the words: "I should like you to be as I am?" And yet,
even if he had not added: "Still, each one has his own
gift,"[110] we could not call him a braggart. Why then has
he added: "as I am?" It is not for self-aggrandizement,
for this is the man who has surpassed the apostles in the
tasks of preaching but who believes himself to be unworthy
of the name of apostle. After he says: "I am the least of
the apostles,"[111] as if he had uttered something exceeding
his own worth, he quickly interrupts himself with the words:
"I do not even deserve the name." Why does he add this
phrase to his exhortation? He has not simply done it without thinking, nor by chance. He knows that students are
especially inspired to emulate what is good when they receive examples of it from their teachers. This is true in
the case of the philosopher who deals in words alone, and
not action: he is of no help to his student. However, the
teacher who can demonstrate that his counsel has first been
acted upon successfully by himself has a profound influence

upon his listener. In addition, Paul demonstrates that he
is free from envy and conceit by his willingness to share
this exceptional virtue with his pupils. He does not seek
to possess it any more than they but wants them to equal
him in every respect.

2. I can also give a third reason. What is it?
This virtue appears difficult to achieve and not within
the reach of the majority. Wishing to demonstrate its extreme accessibility, he presents to all one who has
achieved it, so that people understand that it does not
involve much work and that they themselves might confident-
ly set foot upon this road with him as a guide. Paul does
the same thing elsewhere. When he addresses the Galatians,
he is anxious to free them from their fear of the Law, a
fear that weighed upon them and bound them to the observa-
tion of the ancient customs they found there. What does
he say? "Become like me as I became like you."[112] His
meaning is this: You, the Galatians, could not object that
I have today converted from paganism, and, not knowing the
fear of transgressing the Law, philosophically discuss all
of this with you without any risk. For I myself was once
enslaved as you are. I was subject to the commandments of
the Law. I observed its injunctions. But when the grace
of God shone upon me, I changed completely from that Law
to this. It is no longer a matter of transgression, "since
we have become the subjects of another man."[113] Therefore,
no one could say that I do one thing but advise you to do
another, or that I endanger you while I am safe. If it
were dangerous, I would not have given myself up or have
neglected my own safety. So, just as Paul has eased the
Galatians' anxiety by setting himself out in that passage
as an example, so here he dispels anxiety by presenting
himself for all to see.

XXXVI
The Apostle Calls Virginity
A Divine Gift Out Of Modesty

1. "Still, each one has his own gift from God, one
this and another that."[114] Notice that the characteristic
mark of apostolic humility is lost at no point but shines
through with clarity everywhere. He calls his virtuous
action the gift of God and what he has taken great pains
to do he attributes entirely to his master. Why is it astonishing if he does this in the case of continence when
he adopts a similar tone in his discussion about his
preaching, for which he suffered a thousand hardships,
continual affliction, untold pain and experienced death
each day? What does he say about it? "I have worked harder than all the others, not on my own but through the favor
of God."[115] He does not say it with partly his own efforts,
partly God's, but God's completely. It is the mark of a
faithful servant to think that nothing is his but everything his master's, to believe nothing is his but everything the Lord's.

2. Paul does the same thing elsewhere. After saying: "We have gifts that differ according to the favor be-
stowed on each one of us,"[116] he proceeds to number among
them the gift of administration, of almsgiving and works
of charity. It is evident to all, however, that these are
virtuous acts and not divine favors. I have discussed this
so that whenever you hear Paul say: "Each one has his own
gift," you do not lose heart or tell yourself: there is no
need for my own effort, for Paul has called it a divine
gift. He says this out of modesty, and not because he
wants to number continence among divine gifts. Indeed, he
would not have contradicted in this way both himself and
Christ, who says: "There are some men who have castrated

themselves for the kingdom of heaven," and who adds: "Let
him accept this teaching who can."[117]   Paul himself has
condemned women who chose widowhood but then do not desire to abide by their decision.[118]If it is a gift of God,
why does he threaten them with the words: "This will bring
them condemnation for breaking their first pledge?"   Nowhere did Christ punish those without the gift of grace,
but he always punished those who did not exhibit an upright life.   This is sought above all by him: the most
perfect way of life and conduct above reproach.   The dis-
tribution of divine gifts depends not upon the motive of
the beneficiary but upon the decision of the donor. Christ
accordingly at no point praises those who accomplish miracles.   When his disciples pride themselves on this, he
leads them from such self-satisfaction with the words:
"Do not rejoice...that the devils are subject to you."[119]
For the blessed are always the compassionate, the humble,
the kind, the pure in heart, the peacemakers, those who
perform all of these and similar acts.[120]

     3.   Moreover, Paul himself in counting up his own
acts of virtue has mentioned continence among these. After
saying: "With great endurance, amid trials, difficulties,
distresses, beatings, imprisonment, riots... sleepness
nights, and fastings,"[121] he adds: "in purity," which he
would not have included if that were a gift from God.
Why does he scoff at those lacking this virtue and call
them incontinent?   Why again does the man who does not
marry his virgin do better?[122]   Why is the widow more
blessed if she remains as she is?   As I have already stated,
because the promises of blessedness arise not from miracles
but from actions, which is true of punishments also.   Why
does Paul continually advise the same conduct if the abil-
ity to do it did not lie within us, and if after the inter-
vention of God, there were no need of our own effort?   For

after saying: "I should like you to be as I am," continent, he repeats: "To those not married and to widows I
have this to say: It would be well if they remain as they
are, even as I do myself."[123] Again he sets himself forth
as an example for the same reason: having an example close
by and relevant to them, they would undertake, he thought,
more courageously the tasks of virginity. If he says
above: "I should like you to be as I am," and here: "It
would be well if they remain as they are, even as I do myself," and nowhere gives the reason, do not be surprised.
He is not acting arrogantly but believes that his personal
conviction, by means of which he achieved this virtue, is
sufficient reason.

XXXVII
There Is Much Unpleasantness
In Second Marriages

1. If you want to hear the reasons for this, first
scrutinize public opinion, and then what normally happens.
Although lawmakers in fact do not penalize second marriages
but permit and accept them, much is said against them both
in private and in public. They are mocked, reproached, and
repudiated by many. People turn their back, so to speak,
on those who remarry no less than on perjurors; they dare
neither to make such persons their friends, nor to make
agreements with them, nor to trust them in anything else.
When you see those who have remarried striking so easily
from their hearts the memory of their former loving intimacy, their conjugal relations and life together, a numb-
ness comes over you, and it is impossible to approach them
in all friendship, since they are inconstant and fickle.
And they are avoided not only for these reasons but also
because of the unpleasant nature of the consequences.
2. For, tell me, what is more disagreeable than this

contrast: the sudden reversal from much wailing, lamentation, tears, dissheveled hair and black dress to clapping,
preparations for the bridal chamber, and cheers, all in
sharp contrast to what preceded, like actors playing on
the stage becoming first this character, then that? Indeed, on the stage you would see an actor now as king,
now poorer than everyone else. In this case, the man who
recently was grovelling at the tomb suddenly becomes a
bridegroom. He who was tearing out his hair now wears a
wreath again on the same head. The man with gloomy and
downcast look, who often had tearfully eulogized his dead
wife to those offering consolation, who said life was intolerable for him, who was annoyed at people distracting
him from his grief, often in the midst of all this the
very same man preens and adorns himself once more. With
eyes that were just now tearful he looks laughingly at his
friends and kisses them in greeting with the same mouth
that just now forswore all of this.

3. However, the more pitiful aspect of second marriages is the hostility introduced among the children, the
lioness made to live with the daughters; for everywhere
the mother-in-law is this. From this union stem daily
arguments and fights; from it there arises an unaccustomed
and strange jealousy against the dead wife, who causes no
trouble. For the living both envy and are envied, but we
become reconciled with our dead enemies—but not in this
case. The dead wife's dust and ashes are objects of
jealousy. There is unspeakable hatred against her, although she is buried. Insults, gibes and accusations
arise against the woman who has decomposed in the earth.
Implacable enmity exists against her who has caused no
pain. What is worse than this unreasonableness, this
cruelty? The new wife has suffered no harm from the departed wife—why do I say suffered no harm? She has

reaped the fruits of that woman's labor, and enjoys her
estate; but inspite of this the new wife fights vainly
with her. And this woman who has inflicted no injury,
who has often even never been seen by the new wife, is
each day attacked with countless sarcasms, and through
her children punished even though dead. Her husband too
is frequently pitted against his children when the new
wife has been unsuccessful in this herself. Yet, we find
all of this easy to bear if only we are not forced to endure the tyranny of our lust!

4. The virgin has not lost her head in the face of
this struggle, nor has she escaped the encounter that appears to be intolerable to many. Instead she has nobly
stood firm and undertaken a battle with nature. Then,
how can she be admired as she deserves? Others need second marriages in order not to be consumed, whereas she
touches not even one man and is consistently holy and inviolate. It is for this reason and above all because of
the heavenly wages in store for widowhood that he who has
Christ speaking within has stated: "It would be well if
they remain as they are, even as I do myself."[124] You
are not strong enough to ascend to the highest peak? Do
not fall at least from the next level. Let the virgin
surpass you only to this extent: desire has not once gotten the better of her, but overpowering you at first, it
did not prevail forever. You have won after being de-
feated, whereas she has victory free of every defeat. She
surpasses you only at the start since she reaches the
finish at the same time as you.

XXXVIII
Why Paul Gives So Much Encouragement
To Married People But Gives No
Respite To The Virgin

1. But how can Paul give so much encouragement to
married people by advising that they not deprive one another without mutual consent and that their abstinence,
which arose from mutual consent, not last too long? He
has also permitted a second marriage if they wish it, so
that they not "be on fire."[125] Yet he has given no such
encouragement to virgins. While he restrains married
couples just so far and then lets them renew their relationship, he exposes the virgin. She barely catches her
breath but battles incessantly against a continuous on-
slaught of passion. Not even a small respite is hers.
Why has he not said to her too: if you cannot exercise
self-control, get married? For the same reason you could
no more say to the champion after he has cast aside his
clothes and been anointed with oil, once he has entered
the stadium and been spattered with dust: withdraw, run
from your rival. Instead, the champion is faced with two
choices: either to leave with a crown or having fallen to
retire with dishonor. Indeed, in the gymnasium and wrest-
ling school where there is exercise with associates and
you interlock bodies with friends as rivals, the athlete
himself decides whether to exert himself or not; but after
he is registered and a crowd gathers in the theatre, when
the judge is present and the spectators are seated and the
adversary is brought in to face him, the law of the contest takes precedence over his personal decision.

2. The same applies to the virgin: as long as she
deliberates beforehand whether she ought to marry or not,
marriage poses no threat. When she has made her choice
and is enrolled, she has brought herself into the stadium.

When the theatre has been filled and the angels are watching from above, when Christ is presiding and the devil in a rage gnashes his teeth and, grasping her about the waist, is locked in combat with her, who will dare go into the center and cry out: run from your enemy, give up your efforts, withdraw from his grip, do not throw your rival down or upset him but concede victory to him?

3. What do I say to virgins? No one would dare utter this to widows; in its place one would give this fearful speech: "...when their passions estrange them from Christ they will want to marry. This will bring them condemnation for breaking their first pledge."[126] In fact, Paul himself states that: "To those not married and to widows I have this to say: It would be well if they remain as they are, even as I do myself; but if they cannot exercise self-control, they should marry."[127] And again: "If her husband dies she is free to marry whomever she wishes, but on one condition, that it be in the Lord."[128]

XXXIX
The Widow and Virgin Who Are
Permitted By Paul To Marry

1. How can he chastise the woman whom he lets go free? How can he condemn this marriage that he says is "in the Lord" for being illegitimate? Do not worry. There are two types of marriage under discussion. It is like his statement: "Neither does a virgin commit a sin if she marries;"[129] he is not speaking of a girl who has renounced marriage, for it is apparent to all that she has sinned in an unforgivable way. The statement applies rather to the girl who has not experienced marriage yet, and who has not yet elected either course but remains undecided between the two. He has the same idea with respect to the widow. In the one place, he speaks of a widow simply as a woman

without a husband, and who has not yet committed herself
by making a deliberate choice about her life but who is
free to choose either course. In the other, however, the
widow is no longer entitled to be intimate with another
bridegroom since she has embarked upon the contest of
self-control.

2. For it is possible to be a widow and not be enrolled in the rank of widows, as when a woman has not as
yet accepted this way of life. Accordingly Paul says:
"To be on the church's roll of widows, a widow should not
be less than sixty years of age. She must have been married only once."[130] He allows the uncommitted woman to
remarry if she so desires, but he strongly condemns the
one who has professed perpetual widowhood to God but then
has gotten married because she has treated with contempt
her agreement with God. So, he addresses not to these
widows but those mentioned earlier the remark: "But if
they cannot exercise self-control, they should marry.
It is better to marry than to be on fire."[131] Do you see
that marriage is in no way esteemed for itself but always
as a means of avoiding fornication, temptations and incontinence? He employs all of these terms above in the case
of professed widows; here, after strenuously reproaching
them, he reviews the same matter again using milder language and calls it an inflamation and fire.

3. Yet he has not refrained from dealing a blow to
his audience in passing. He has not said for instance:
if they experience any violent passion, if they are carried away, if they are unable. He says nothing of the
kind, which would be proper for those who suffer and deserve sympathy. What does he say? "If they cannot exercise self-control," which applies to those not wanting to
make the effort because of their apathy. He points out
that although they are masters of the situation, through

their disinclination to work they do not succeed. Nevertheless, he neither punishes them nor considers them li-
able for punishment, but he deprives them of praise and
demonstrates his severity only in his expression of censure. Nowhere has he mentioned the procreation of children, the specious and grand reason for marriage; instead
he cites being "on fire," incontinence, fornication, temptations of the devil—to avoid them he agrees to marriage.

4. —What of this, you say: as long as marriage de-
livers us from punishment, we will easily bear every condemnation and reproach, provided only that it is possible
to live riotously and to indulge our passions without
interruption. —But what if, my good man, it is not permitted to run riot, will we be censured only? —You reply,
how is it forbidden to live so when Paul declares: "But if
they cannot exercise self-control, they should marry?"[132]

5. But hear also what follows this statement. You
have learned that it is better to marry than to be on
fire. You have approved what was agreeable to you. You
have applauded the conciliatory tone. You have admired
the apostle for his indulgence. Do not stop there. Accept the rest also, for both precepts come from the same
man. What does Paul add? "To those now married, however,
I give this command (though it is not mine; it is the
Lord's); a wife must not separate from her husband. If
she does separate, she must either remain single or become
reconciled to him again. Similarly, a husband must not
divorce his wife."[133]

XL
The Bondage Of Marriage
Heavy And Inevitable

1. What if a husband is moderate but his wife is
wicked, carping, a chatterbox, extravagant (the affliction

common to all womankind), filled with many other faults,
how will that poor fellow endure this daily unpleasantness,
this conceit, this impudence? What if she is discreet and
gentle, on the other hand, but he is rash, contemptuous,
irascible, putting on airs either because of his wealth or
his power? What if he treats her as a slave, though she
is free, and considers her no better than the maids-in-
waiting? How will she endure such duress and violence?
What if he continually neglects her and persists in doing
so? Paul says to bear this bondage patiently, for you
will be free only when he dies; while he lives there are
necessarily two choices: either take great pains and
train him or, if this is impossible, endure nobly this
unproclaimed war, this battle without a truce.

2. He stated earlier: "Do not deprive one another,
unless perhaps by mutual consent.[134] Here he bids a woman
who has been separated to exercise self-control henceforth
even against her will. "She must either remain single,"
he says, "or become reconciled to him."[135] Do you see
that she has been caught in the middle? She must either
master the violence of her passion or, unwilling to do
this, flatter her overbearing lord, and submit herself to
whatever he wishes, whether he strikes her or bathes her
in abuse or exposes her to the contempt of the household
or the like.

3. Many methods have been devised by husbands when
they want to punish their wives. If the wife cannot endure it, she must practice an unprofitable self-control.
I say unprofitable in as much as she has not the proper
purpose, for it arises not out of a desire for holiness
but out of anger at her husband. "She must either remain
single or become reconciled to him." What if he refuses
reconciliation forever? You have a second solution and
way out. What is it? Wait for him to die.

4. If a virgin is never permitted to marry, this
is not the case with married women when their husbands
have died. If, in fact, it were possible even while the
first husband lived to flit from him to another, and
again from the second to a third, what would the purpose
of marriage be when men would have access to the wives
of others indiscriminately, and there would simply be
general promiscuity? Would not our attitude towards our
companions be ruined, if today this man, tomorrow that,
and then others live with the same woman? Therefore, the
Lord has rightly called this adultery.[136]

XLI
Why God Has Granted The Practice
Of Divorce To The Jews

1. Why, then, has this been granted to the Jews?
Clearly because of their hardness of heart,[137] so that
they not fill their houses with the bloodshed of kinsmen.
For, tell me, what would have been better: that the hated
woman be driven out or that she be slain at home? For
they would have done this if it were impossible to divorce their wives. This is why Scripture says: "If you
despise her, send her away."[138] But when Paul addresses
reasonable people to whom he does not concede even anger,[139] what does he say? "If she does separate, she
must...remain single."[140] Do you perceive the duress
and the inexorable bondage, the fetters encircling each
of them? For marriage truly is a chain, not only because
of the multitude of its anxieties and daily worries, but
also because it forces spouses to submit to one another,
which is harsher than every other kind of servitude.

2. "He shall be your master."[141] What is the advantage of this supremacy? For, in turn, God makes the
husband her slave. He has designed a strange and sur-

prising exchange of bondage. It is like fugitive slaves
who have been bound by their masters first separately,
then to one another, each pair fastened at their feet by
a short chain: they are unable to walk independently because each must follow the other. Thus, the souls of
married couples have both their own private cares and a
second constraint arising from the bond between them. It
strangles them more fiercely than any chain. It robs
them both of freedom by not offering to one alone supremacy but divides the authority between them. Where, then,
are those ready to endure every condemnation in return
for consolation from sexual pleasure?

3. For, with the passage of time, no small part of
pleasure is often diminished amid mutual anger and hatred.
By forcing one spouse to involuntarily endure the baseness
of the other, this servitude is sufficient to obscure
every joy. Therefore, St. Paul at first checked the onset
of lust with words fit to make anyone feel ashamed; he
says "to avoid immorality, incontinence and burning desire.[142] When he saw that condemnation meant little to
most people, he increased the severity of his tone in order to dissuade them, which made his pupils say: "It is
better not to marry."[143] There is this statement too:
"No spouse belongs to himself."[144] Paul no longer presents this as advice and counsel, but as an order and command. Whether we marry or not depends upon us; but enduring its servitude, not willingly but unwillingly, does
not depend upon us.

4. Why is that? Because we chose this slavery to
begin with not in ignorance but knowing full well its
claims and laws. We willingly put ourselves under its
yoke. Then, after discussing those who live with unbelievers, after precisely listing all the regulations concerning marriage, after inserting his words about the

slaves[145] and encouraging them sufficiently that their
spiritual nobility was not diminished by this slavery,
Paul arrives finally at his theme of virginity. Before
this he was in labor, eager to spread his thoughts abroad.
Now he has given birth (although he could not bear keeping silent about it in his treatment of marriage).

   5. Paul has woven his theme of virginity briefly
and in passing into his recommendation to marry. By this
excellent method he prepares his audience by smoothing
the way for their understanding and providing the best
introduction to his discussion. Accordingly, following
his exhortation to the slaves (for he says: "You have
been bought at a price! Do not enslave yourselves to
men"[146]), after he has reminded us of the benefits received from the Lord and in this way has raised and
lifted everyone's thoughts toward heaven, then does he
introduce his discussion of virginity. He says: "With
respect to virgins, I have not received any commandment
from the Lord, but I give my opinion, as one who is
trustworthy, thanks to the Lord's mercy."[147] And yet,
even though you do not have the Lord's commandment concerning the marriage of the faithful to unbelievers, with
great authority you, Paul, have framed this rule when
you write: "As for the other matters, although I know
nothing the Lord has said, I say: If any brother has a
wife who is an unbeliever but is willing to live with
him, he must not divorce her."[148] Then why do you not
make a similar declaration about virgins? Because on
this point Christ has openly indicated his will, preventing virginity from becoming obligatory. For the statement, "Let him accept this teaching who can,"[149] endows
the listener with the power to choose. So when he discusses continence, Paul says: "I should like you to be
as I am,"[150] continent, and again: "To those not married

and to widows I have this to say: It would be well if
they remain as they are, even as I do myself."[151]   But at
no time in this discourse on virginity has he introduced
himself. With great reserve and humility he addresses
the subject, for he himself did not accomplish this goal
successfully. "I have not received any commandment from
the Lord," he says.[152]

7. Paul gives his listener a choice at first and
makes him receptive, and so introduces his counsel. Since
the word virginity once stated immediately reveals the
great effort involved, he has not rushed headlong into
his exhortation. No, he first flatters his pupil by offering him a choice and so renders his soul obedient and
docile, then introduces his subject. You have heard the
term virginity, which implies great pains and effort. Do
not be afraid; there is no command nor the constraint of
an injunction. Virginity repays with its own rewards
those who willingly and deliberately accept it. It places
its radiant and flowering crown upon their heads. Yet
those who decline and are unwilling to accept it are
neither punished nor compelled against their wills to
practice it.

8. This is not the only way in which Paul has made
his speech agreeable and not tiresome. He has accomplished this also by revealing that this manifestation of
grace comes not from him but from Christ. He has not
said: with respect to virgins, I do not issue an order,
but "I have not received any commandment from the Lord,"[153]
as if he were saying: if I were recommending this virtue
on the basis of conclusions drawn from human reasoning,
there would be no need for confidence; however, since it
seemed good to God, the guarantee of the freedom of choice
is assured. I have been deprived of the authority to make
such commands, but if you wish to hear me as a fellow-

servant, I say, "I give my opinion as one who is trustworthy, thanks to the Lord's mercy."

9. It is appropriate to admire here the apostle's
great skill and wisdom; how, caught between two conflicting necessities—that of composing his expression so as
to make his advice acceptable, and that of not boasting
in view of his own neglect of this virtue—he has accomplished both in a few words. By saying "thanks to the
Lord's mercy," he commends himself somehow, but by doing
this in an unostentatious manner, he humbles himself once
more by his self-effacement.

XLII
About Paul's Humility

1. He did not say: I give my opinion as one entrusted with the gospel, as one deemed worthy of preaching to the Gentiles, as one charged with leading you, as
your teacher and instructor.[154] What does he say? "As
one who is trustworthy, thanks to the Lord's mercy,"[155]
thereby diminishing his own importance; for being merely
trustworthy is less important than being the teacher of
the faithful. He also thinks of another form of self-
abasement. What is it? He has not said: as one who is
trustworthy, but "as one who is trustworthy, thanks to
the Lord's mercy." It is as if he said: do not think
that only my apostolate, preaching and instruction spring
from God's bounty, for faith itself came to me from his
mercy. It was not because I was deserving, he says,
I was deemed worthy of faith; I owe that to his mercy.
But mercy arises from grace and has nothing to do with
one's worthiness.

2. So, if God were not extremely tender-hearted,
not only would I have been unable to be an apostle but I
would not have been even a believer. Do you observe the

candor of the servant and his contriteness of heart? Do
you see how he attributes nothing more to himself than to
the others? Even the faith that was common to the disciples he says sprung not from him but from God's mercy
and grace. With these words he makes the same point, as
if he were saying: Do not disdain my advice, for God has
not deemed me unworthy of his mercy. Anyway, it is my
opinion, not a command; for I give advice but do not leg-
islate. But no law would forbid bringing forward and pro-
posing what helps each man, especially when this occurs
at the request of the listener, as in your case. Therefore he says: "It seems good to me for a person to continue as he is."[156] Again, do you notice the reserved
tone of his words, free of every indication of authority?
And yet he could have expressed himself so: in as much as
the Lord did not command virginity, neither do I. But I
do recommend it to you and urge you to strive after it,
for I am your apostle.

     3. And this would go along with what he says to them
later: "Although I may not be an apostle for others, I
certainly am one for you."[157] But here he has uttered
nothing of the kind. He speaks very discreetly. Instead
of saying: "I advise," he says: "I give my own opinion;"
instead of: "as a teacher," "as one who is trustworthy,
thanks to the Lord's mercy." And as if this were not
sufficient to humble his speech, from the start he once
again minimizes his authority by not simply declaring his
advice but by giving the reason too. For he says: "In
the present time of stress it seems good to me for a person to continue as he is."[158] However, in his discussion
of continence, he has set down neither the words "I think"
nor any reason but simply stated: "It would be well if
they remain as they are, even as I do myself";[159] but
here: "In the present time of stress it seems good to me

for a person to continue as he is." He does so not out
of doubt—far from it!—but out of his desire to rely
completely upon the judgement of his audience. For the
counselor does not himself vote on what was said but
leaves the decision entirely up to his audience.

XLIII
What Paul Means By Present Stress

What sort of stress does he speak of here? Is it,
then, physical stress? Not at all. In the first place,
if he had meant this, he would have brought about the opposite of what he wished by mentioning it, since those
who wish to marry twist this statement inside out. In
the second place, he would not have called this drive
"present." It was not implanted in the race of men now
for the first time, but at the beginning, and it was in
days gone by more acute and intractable; but after the
coming of Christ and the bestowal of virtue besides, it
has become manageable. So Paul means not this but intimates something else that has many varied and multifold
forms. What is it then? The perversity of things in
this life. For so great is the confusion, so great the
tyranny of cares, so great the multitude of misfortune
that the married man frequently against his will is compelled to sin and go wrong.

XLIV
It Is Easier To Obtain The Kingdom
Of Heaven Through Virginity Than
Through Marriage

1. Formerly, in fact, so strict a standard of virtue was not in force. Vengeance was permissible as was
answering insult with insult, handling money, swearing,
exacting an eye for an eye, and hating one's enemy; neither living luxuriously nor growing angry nor divorcing

one wife and substituting another had been prohibited.
This is not all. The law permitted having two wives at
once. The concessions were many in these and all other
areas. But after the advent of Christ the path became
much narrower, not only because of the curtailment of this
extraordinary freedom of our own authority in all the
areas cited, but also because we at all times keep at home
the woman who frequently seduces us and forces us against
our will to commit innumerable sins or we stand convicted
of adultery if we wish to divorce her.

    2. This is not the only reason why virtue is hard
for us to attain; even if our spouse has a tolerable dis-
position, the plethora of cares surrounding us because of
her and her children gives us little time to look heaven-
ward, as if our souls were submerged from all sides by a
whirling turmoil. Take the case of a man who desires a
life of privacy free from danger and the troubles of business and politics: when he sees his children in a bad way
and his wife in need of spending money, he unwillingly
throws himself into the affairs of state. Once he stum-
bles in that arena it is impossible to count further how
many sins he is forced to commit: he develops a temper,
he grows arrogant, he swears, he makes abusive comments,
he dissembles, doing much for the sake of a favor, much
out of hatred. How is it possible for him, buffeted as
he is by so great a storm and wishing to distinguish himself in it, not to be stained by sin? And if you examine
his household affairs, you will discover them to be full
of the same difficulties, even more, because of his wife.
For a husband must attend to the numerous details of many
things, which he would not have to if he were single.
And this is true when the woman is discreet and reasonable.
But if she is wicked, burdensome and hard to control, we
will no longer call marriage a necessity, but punishment

and chastisement! How will a man be able to walk along
the road to heaven, which requires feet nimble and un-
fettered and a soul unencumbered and well-equipped, if
he has such troubles hanging over him, if he has been
bound by such shackles, dragged down continually by such
a chain, by which I mean the wickedness of his wife?

XLV
No Wage Is In Store For
Those Devising Excessive
Trials For Themselves

1. But what is the knowing reply of many people to
all the difficulties wc have ennumerated to them? Is it
not that success in the midst of such great constraint
means a greater compensation? —Why is that, my good man?
—Because you endure greater hardship from marriage.
—And who compelled you to assume so great a burden? For
if marriage were in compliance with an order and not marrying were a violation of the law, this reasoning would
be sound at first glance. But, having the choice of not
passing under the yoke of marriage, if you willingly and
without compulsion had wanted to take on such difficulties
to make the contest for virtue more strenuous, this is of
no matter to the judge. He has imposed upon us one duty only:
success in the battle against the devil and victory over
evil. Whether you accomplish this through marriage and
luxurious living and attention to many details or through
asceticism and the endurance of hardship, indifferent to
all else, this matters little to him. For the path to
victory and the road leading us to the trophy, he says,
is that one free of all human concerns.

2. But you wish to have a wife and children and all
that they entail, and so take the field and do battle to
accomplish the same results as those who have been en-

tangled in none of this,—and you wish to be admired more
on account of this? Perhaps now you will accuse us of
great conceit if we say that you will be incapable of
reaching the same level as they. But the result of the
competition and the moment of crowning the victor will
convince you soon enough that security is far better than
empty ambition and it is better to obey Christ than the
vanity of one's own thoughts.[160] For Christ says that to
be virtuous it is not enough to renounce one's goods unless we also hate ourselves.[161] You said that you would
prevail, even though you are mixed up in all of these affairs. Yet, as I have said, you will understand clearly
at that time how great an impediment to virtue is a wife
and your attention to her.

XLVI
If A Wife Is An Impediment To The
Perfect Life, Why Does The Scriptures
Call Her A Helper Of Her Husband?

1. How then, you will say, could have God called
this impediment a helper? Indeed he says: "Let us make
for him a helper like himself."[162] Yet, I ask you how
does she help who deprives her husband of so much security,
who banished him from that splendid life in Paradise, and
who has thrown him into the confusion of the present life?
This is not help but treachery. Scripture says: "In woman
was sin's beginning,/ and because of her we all die."[163]
Saint Paul says: "...it was not Adam who was deceived but
the woman."[164]

2. How could she be a helper who subjected man to
death? How could she be a helper through whom the sons
of God, or rather all the inhabitants of the earth at that
time, along with the beasts, birds and all the other creatures perished engulfed in a flood? Would not a woman

have destroyed the just Job, if he had not been so much
of a man?[165] Did not a woman destroy Samson?[166] Was it
not a woman who caused the nation of the Hebrews to be
initiated into the cult of Beelphegor and to be massacred
at the hands of kinsmen?[167] A woman above all who delivered Ahab to the devil,[168] and before him, Solomon,
after his life of renowned wisdom and good repute?[169]
Do not women still today convince their husbands to give
much offence to God? For this reason does not the sage
say: "There is scarce any evil like that in a woman?"[170]

        3. How then could God have said to man: "Let us
make for him a helper like himself?"[171] For God does not
lie. Nor would I assert this, far from it. Although
woman did come into being for this purpose and this reason, she did not want to keep to her dignified state,
just as her husband did not. God made man after his own
image and likeness. He says: "Let us make man in our own
image, after our likeness,"[172] just as he has said: "Let
us make a helper for him." Yet once he was created, man
immediately lost both traits. He did not preserve the
"after God's image" or "after God's likeness." Really
how could he when he gave into unnatural desire and, powerless in the face of pleasure, was caught by a trick?
Against his will the image was taken from him from that
time on.

        4. God cut man off from no small share of his
power, namely, that of being feared by all as a master,
as if God had created him an ungrateful slave who, after
giving offence to his master, is despicable to his fellow-
slaves. For at the beginning man inspired fear in all the
animals, since God turned all over to him. None dared to
maltreat him or plot against him, for they saw the kingly
image shining in him. When man obscured those character-
istics by his sin, God took that power from him.

    5. The fact that man is not in command of all upon
the earth but even trembles before and fears some creatures does not make a lie of God's assertion: "And let
them be the rulers of the beasts of the earth,"[173] for
the curtailment of man's power has come about not from
the donor but from the receiver. Likewise, the plots
originating from women against men have no effect on that
pronouncement that says: "Let us make a helper for him
like himself." Woman in fact did come into existence for
this purpose but she did not adhere to it. Apart from
this, it is possible to say with regard to the arrange-
ment of present life and the procreation of children and
physical desires, she displays the help that is her very
own. But when it is no longer a matter of present life,
or of child-rearing, or of desire, why do you futilely
mention her as a helper? For a woman is capable only of
being of service in the least important matters: if someone were to introduce her as an associate in the most important matters, not only would she be of no help, she
would even enmesh him in cares.

                          XLVII
                  How Woman Is A Helper
                   In Spiritual Things

    1. What then, you say, will we reply to Paul when
he asks: "Wife, how do you know that you will save your
husband?"[174] But does he not also declare her support is
necessary even in spiritual matters? I certainly concur
in this. I do not say she is of no help altogether in
spiritual matters (indeed no!), but I do assert that she
successfully accomplishes this not when she is involved
with marital concerns but when she progresses to the virtue of the holy men while adhering to her feminine nature.
For it is not by beautifying herself, or by living a life

of luxury, or by demanding from her husband money, or by
being extravagant and lavish that she will be able to win
him over. When she removes herself from all present concerns and imprints upon herself the apostolic way of life,
when she displays great modesty, decorum, disdain for
money and forbearance, then will she be able to capture
him. When she says: "If we have food and clothing we
have all that we need,"[175] when she practices this philosophy in her actions and, laughing at physical death, calls
this life nothing, when she considers along with the prophet every glory of this life to be as the flower of the
field,[176] then she will capture him.

    2. Not by living with him as a wife will she be
able to save her husband, but by pointing out to him life
according to the gospel and yet many women have done this
without marrying. For example, Priscilla, it is said, won
over Apollos and led him by the hand all along the road
of truth.[177] If now this is not permitted, it is possible
in the case of wives to display the same zeal and enjoy
the same advantage. In fact, as I have said already, a
woman does not influence a man by being his wife, since
then there would be nothing preventing a man with a be-
lieving wife from converting, if a conjugal and communal
life accomplished this result. But this is not so, no.
The display of a grand philosophy and much patience, the
scoffing at the misfortunes of marriage, and the determi-
nation to follow this task through from beginning to end,
this is to make the soul of one's companion safe; but if
she continues making the demands of wives, she would not
help him but even harm him. The matter involves serious
difficulties. Hear what Paul says: "Wife, how do you know
that you will save your husband?"[178] We have become accustomed to using this manner of questioning in matters
occurring contrary to expectation.

3.   After this what does he say? "Are you bound to
a wife? Then do not seek your freedom. Are you free of
a wife? If so, do not go in search of one."[179] Do you
see how he continually shifts, creating a mixture of both
recommendations within a short space of time? As in his
discourse on marriage when he introduced remarks on continence and in the process aroused his listeners' interest,
so even here he introduces remarks about marriage again
and gives his audience a respite. He began with virginity
but before saying anything about it immediately, he has
reverted to his speech about marriage. For the phrase,
"I do not have his command," comes from a man who accedes
to and admits marriage. Then, after coming to the topic
of virginity and saying that: "I think this is a good
state," since he has observed that its name repeated constantly causes delicate ears to bristle, he does not mention it frequently. Although with this phrase he has
given sufficient reason to encourage making the effort on
behalf of virginity, namely present necessity, he has not
dared to repeat the word virginity. What does he say?
"...it seems good to me for a person to continue as he is."
And he does not develop further his thought. He stops
short and interrupts himself before it appears obtrusive.
He begins again to speak about marriage: "Are you bound
to a wife? Then do not seek your freedom." Obviously,
if it were not there his purpose, if he did not intend
here to encourage his listener, it would have been unnecessary to philosophize about marriage if he wished to recommend virginity. And then he returns to virginity, but
again he does not call it by its proper name. What does he
say? "Are you free of a wife? If so, do not go in search
of one."

4.   Do not fear. He has not made a flat declaration
or legislated a law. For his words about marriage stand

nearby again. He dismisses this fear with these words:
"Should you marry, you will not be committing a sin."[180]
But do not lose heart now, for he draws you back to virginity. This is the purpose of his speech, to teach us
that there awaits much affliction for the flesh for those
intent upon marriage. Paul is like the finest gentle phy-
sicians who, about to introduce a bitter remedy such as a
drug or surgery or cautery or the like, do not perform
every step all at once but give to the patient a breathing
spell and then apply the rest. In the same fashion, Saint
Paul, too, does not weave his advice on virginity without
pause as a whole piece with each point in succession. Instead, he continually interrupts it with words on marriage
and by depriving virginity of its extreme aspects renders
his speech soothing and acceptable. The intricate mixture
of his words has come about for this reason.

5. It is worthwhile also to scrutinize the phrases
themselves. "Are you bound to a wife?" he asks, "then do
not seek your freedom." This is not advice so much as an
indication of the difficult and inescapable nature of the
bond. Why has he *not* said: "Do you have a wife? Do not
forsake her. Live with her. Do not stand apart from her."
Instead he has called the yoke a bond. He does this to
demonstrate the burdensome nature of the state of marriage.
For inasmuch as everyone rushes into marriage as if it were
a welcome institution, he shows that married couples differ
in no way from prisoners. And in this case wherever one
pulls, the other must follow or disagreeing he must perish
with the other. You ask, what if my husband is morally
depraved but I wish to be continent? You must follow him.
Indeed, the chain encircling you thanks to marriage drags
you down, although you are unwilling, and pulls you to him
who was bound to you in the beginning. If you resist and
break out, not only do you not release yourself from the

the chains, you even expose yourself to extreme punishment.

XLVIII
The Wife Who Is Continent Contrary To The Wish Of Her Husband Will Pay a Greater Penalty Than He If He Commits Adultery

1.   The wife practicing continence against her husband's wishes is deprived of the rewards for continence. She also has to give account for his adultery and is more responsible than he. Why? Because she pushed him to the abyss of debauchery by depriving him of legitimate intercourse. For if this conduct has not been approved even for a short period of time, if the husband is unwilling, what forgiveness can she expect who robs him continually of this consolation? You will ask what could be harsher than this constraint and despiteful treatment? I agree with you. Why then do you subject yourself to so great a constraint? You should have reasoned in this way not after marriage but before.

2.   This is why Paul sets forth next the constraint arising from the bond and then discusses the means of deliverance from it. After stating: "Are you bound to a wife? Then do not seek your freedom," he then adds, "Are you free of a wife? If so, do not go in search of one." He does this so that you reflect carefully and examine closely beforehand the strength of this yoke and accept more readily his thoughts on celibacy. "Should you marry," he says, "you will not be committing a sin. Neither does a virgin commit a sin, if she marries." Behold where the fine virtue of marriage leads: you are not accused, nor are you admired. Admiration is reserved for virginity, but the married man is satisfied hearing that he has not sinned. Why then, you say, do you recommend not looking for a wife? Because it is not possible to be released once you have

been enchained, because marriage involves much affliction.
Tell me, do we gain then only this from virginity, the
avoidance of affliction here and now? Who will submit to
virginity for such wages? Who would be content, as he is
about to descend to so great a struggle filled with so
much sweat, to receive this recompense only?

XLIX
Why Paul Directs Us From Pleasures
In This Life To Virginity

1. What do you say? Do you invite me to do battle
with the devils?——"Our battle is not against human forces."[181]
——Do you urge me to stand firm against the fury of nature?
Do you exhort me to accomplish this with incorporeal powers
though I am but flesh and blood? Do you mention the good
things on earth and say we will not have troubles arising
from marriage? Why has Paul said: if the virgin marries,
she has not sinned but has deprived herself of the crown of
virginity, of presents great and unspeakable? Why has he
not fully described the blessings in store for virgins
after immortality: How taking up torches they come to the
meeting with much glory and confidence, and enter with the
king the bridal chamber?[182] How they especially are radiant by his throne and royal bridal chamber?[182] But the
apostle has not even briefly mentioned these rewards. From
start to finish he only calls to mind the release from
life's annoyances: "...it seems good to me," he says, "for
a person to continue as he is."[183] While he neglects to
say this is because of future blessings, he does say: "Because of present necessity." Then again, after stating:
"Neither does a virgin commit a sin if she marries,"[184]
and passing over in silence the heavenly gifts that she has
deprived herself of, he states: "But people will have
trials in this life."

2. He follows this pattern of discourse all the way
to the conclusion. He does not introduce the topic of
virginity from the point of view of future compensations
but has recourse again to the same reasoning: "...the time
is short,"[185] he observes. Instead of saying: I want you
to be brilliant in heaven and appear much brighter
than married persons, he sticks to the here and now in his
speech: "I should like you to be free of all worries."[186]
He does this here and also in his discussion of patient
endurance, in which he follows the same avenue of advice.
After saying: "If your enemy is hungry, feed him; if he is
thirsty, give him something to drink,"[187] after imposing
so great a duty upon us, after bidding us to overcome the
necessity of nature and to stand prepared against so intolerable a fire, he is silent about heaven and the rewards there when he speaks about compensations. He estab-
lishes that the compensation lies in the harm done to him
causing the pain: "...by doing this," he says, "you will
heap burning coals upon his head."[188]

3. Why has he employed this type of appeal? Not
because of ignorance, nor because he did not know how you
win over and persuade a listener, but because he, above
all others, had achieved this art, I mean that of persua-
sion. The proof? From his words. But in what way? In
his address to the Corinthians—we will first speak about
his discussion of virginity—to the Corinthians, among
whom he resolved that he would acknowledge nothing except
Jesus Christ and him crucified,[189] whom he was unable to
address as spiritual men, to whom he gave milk to drink
since they were still of the flesh, and whom even when
commanding this he accused with the words: "I fed you with
milk and did not give you solid food because you were not
ready for it. You are not ready for it even now, being
still very much in a natural condition."[190]

4. This is why with earthly things, with what is
visible and perceptible he directs them to virginity, and
leads them from marriage. He was well aware that one
could more easily attract and persuade with earthly considerations the faint-hearted, the unspiritual and those
still stooping down to the earth. Tell me why in fact do
many of the more rustic and dull-witted types swear and
forswear by God without fear in small matters as well as
large, but they would prefer never to swear on the heads
of their children? Although the false oath and the punishment are far more serious in the first case, nevertheless
they are restrained more by the second oath than the first.

5. Words about the kingdom of heaven do not incite
them to help the poor, although they are instructed continually to do so, as much as the hope of some advantage
in this life for either themselves or their children. At
any rate, men become especially generous in such assistance
to others whenever they have recovered from a long illness,
or they escape danger, or they gain some powerful position
and office. Generally, we find that the majority of men
are more impressed by what is in front of them. In times
of prosperity this influences them more; in times of ad-
versity this alarms them much more, because the perception
of both states is more immediate for them. Paul accordingly addressed the Corinthians in this way, and trained the
Romans away from present considerations toward the practice
of patient endurance.

6. The weak and injured soul does not in fact so
readily give up its poisonous anger when it hears of the
kingdom of heaven and faces long-term expectations, as when
it thinks that it will exact vengeance for an offence. So,
wishing to root out the memory of past injuries and to
render in the meantime one's anger ineffectual, Paul pro-
poses what was more likely to encourage the injured party.

He does not withhold the future reward, but he is anxious
to lead him in the meantime by such means to the road of
philosophy, and to open the doors for him to reconciliation. For the most difficult part of attaining virtue is
at the beginning. After that, the effort is not so
strenuous.

7. Our Lord Jesus Christ, however, does not discuss virginity nor long-suffering in this way. There he
presents the kingdom of heaven: "There are some men who
have castrated themselves for the sake of the kingdom of
Heaven."[191] Yet, when he calls upon us to pray for our
enemies, Christ makes no mention of harm coming to those
who have caused injury, nor of burning embers. He passes
over all this, which is addressed to the mean-spirited
and miserable, and guides his listeners with more important considerations. What are they? "So that you become
like your father in heaven."[192] Observe how great the
prize is! Indeed, Peter heard this; so did Jacob, John,
and the rest of the apostles. This is why he persuaded
them with spiritual prizes. Paul would have also followed
this method, if he had addressed any of them; but when he
spoke to the Corinthians, being as they were to a greater
degree unperfect, he presents them directly with the fruit
of their labor, so that they may come more readily to the
practice of virtue.

8. For this reason God neglected to proclaim to the
Jews the kingdom of heaven, while he did offer them freely
temporal goods. In return for their wickedness, he threatened not hell but misfortunes in this life, such as famine,
pestilence, disease, war, captivity, and so forth. Men
more carnal in nature are deterred by these things, which
inspire a greater fear in them. They consider less signi-
ficant what cannot be seen here and now. So Paul dwells
in greater length on what was especially able to penetrate

their insensibility. He wanted to demonstrate in addition
that some virtues impose upon us much work here but store
up for the future every reward. Virginity on the other
hand repays us even while it is being achieved with sub-
stantial returns because it releases us from so much work
and anxiety. Moreover, Paul has furnished a third argument for it. What is it? That virginity is not impossible
to attain, but rather very accessible. He does so by
making it abundantly clear that marriage involves more
difficulties. It is as if he said to someone: does virginity seem to you to be troublesome and laborious? Indeed, I say it is necessary to pursue it for this reason:
it is so easy to embrace that it offers far fewer burdens
than marriage. Since I want to spare you, he says, and do
not want you to be sorely tried, I wish that you not marry.

9. Perhaps some will ask what sort of trials these are,
for on the contrary, we will discover in marriage much
license and luxurious living. First of all, there is amid
every indulgence satisfaction of one's passion without
having to endure violent physical drives, which is of no
small importance for one's ease! Then, with the release
of the other aspects of life from sorrow and squalor, life
is filled with joyousness, laughter and delight! Indeed,
with a lavish table, soft clothes, softer bed, continuous
baths, perfume, wine not inferior to the perfume, and many
other various expenses married persons minister to the
flesh and provide it with much luxury!

L
Luxurious Living Is Unlawful Under
Both The Old And The New Law

1. First of all these excesses are not permitted to
marriage. Marriage customarily provides us with the freedom for intercourse only and not for a life of luxury. St.

Paul says: "She who gives herself up to selfish indulgence, however, leads a life of living death."[193] If this is said about widows, hear what he says about married people: "Similarly, the women must deport themselves properly. They should dress modestly and quietly, and not be decked out in fancy hairstyles, gold ornaments, pearls or costly clothing; rather, as becomes women who profess to be religious, their adornment should be good deeds."[194] Here and elsewhere you can see he speaks at length against wanting these things so much.

    2. For he says: "If we have food and clothing we have all that we need. Those who want to be rich are falling into temptation and a trap. They are letting themselves be captured by foolish and harmful desires which drag men down to ruin and destruction."[195] Why do I mention Paul who said this when it was the time of the highest philosophy, when there was grace from the Spirit? For Amos the prophet speaking to the childish Jews, in whose time luxurious living, wealth and all superfluous things, so to speak, were allowed——hear how vehemently he upbraids the devotees of luxury: "Woe to those who approach the evil day, who draw near and celebrate false sabbaths, who sleep on ivory beds and revel on their couches. Woe to those who eat kids taken from the flock and sucking calves from the middle of the herd. Woe to those who clap to the sound of musical instruments. Woe to those who drink strained wine and annoint themselves with the best ointment. They think of these things as lasting and not fleeting."[196]

LI

**Even If It Were Permitted To Live Luxuriously,
The Pain Marriage Brings Is Enough
To Destroy This Pleasure**

    As I said then, it was not permitted to live luxur-

iously in the first place; but even if none of this had
been prohibited and all had been approved, there are more
pressing considerations with regard to marriage that involve despair and mental anguish; or rather, these considerations are so much more numerous and serious that we do
not perceive the slightest advantage in such luxury. It
is devoid of all pleasure.

LII

How Great An Evil Jealousy Is

1. If someone should happen to be jealous by nature
or be caught in this evil through false suspicion, tell me,
what could be more pitiful than such a soul? What war,
what storm compares at all precisely to such a dwelling?
This house is completely filled with pain, suspicion, discord and trouble. The man struck by this madness is no
better off than those possessed or afflicted with a disease
of the brain, so incessantly does he jump up and then sink
back. He is annoyed at one and all and he continually un-
leashes his anger at those who are simply present but
guiltless, whether it be a slave, a son or whoever. All
pleasure has been banished. Everything is filled with sorrow, grief and unpleasantness. Whether he stays at home or
rushes to the marketplace or sets out on a trip abroad,
everywhere he gives way to this dreadful emotion, more
grievous than any death. It makes him jealous, irritating
his soul, not letting it be still. This disease usually
produces an insufferable temper along with despondency.
Each of these is sufficient by itself to destroy its cap-
tive. Endlessly harassing him and not granting him even a
short respite for breath, when they join forces and together besiege their foe, how many deaths would be more terrible than this? If you cite extreme poverty, an incurable disease, fires, the sword, your name nothing equal

to this. Only those who have undergone this experience
understand it well, for no description could represent the
excessive nature of this fearsome emotion. When a man is
forever compelled to suspect the woman he loves more than
all others, for whom he would gladly give up even his life,
what in the world could console him?

2. If he must go to bed or eat or drink, he will
imagine the fare laced with lethal drugs rather than eat-
ables. In bed he will not stop trembling for even a little
while but will toss about in distress as though on a bed of
coals. Neither the companionship of friends nor keeping
busy with his business nor the fear of danger nor abundant
pleasures nor anything else will be able to lessen his distress. This storm rules over his soul more tyrannically
than every kindness or vexation. When Solomon examined
this situation, he said: "Relentless as death is jealousy."[197]
And again: "For vindictive is the husband's wrath; he will
have no pity on the day of vengeance;/ he will not consider
any restitution, nor be satisfied with the greatest gifts."[198]

3. Indeed the madness of this disease is so great
that not even after revenge is exacted upon the party responsible for the injury is one released from mental anguish.
In any case, many men often have not the power to put an end
to their anger and despair although they have killed the
adulterer. And there are some who even after murdering
their own wives remain as they were or are consumed to a
greater degree by this fire. The husband lives with all
these hardships even when there happens to be no truth to
his suspicions; but the wretched and miserable wife endures
much harsher treatment than her husband. For when she sees
the man who ought to be her consolation in all times of
sorrow and from whom she must expect support being more
brutal and hostile to her than any one else, where can she
look in the future? To whom can she flee for protection?

Where can she find deliverance from these troubles when her
harbor has become choked with mud and is filled with thousands of rocks?

4.   Then do the servants and handmaids treat her
more insolently than her husband.   This class is to be suspected and is ungrateful besides, but when it acquires
greater outspokenness, when it sees its masters quarrelling
with each other, it uses that discord as a fine pretext for
its own abusive conduct.   For then it is possible for servants to invent and fabricate as much as they want completely unafraid, and in this way do they increase the at-
mosphere of suspicion with their slander.   For the soul
once afflicted by this miserable disease easily believes
everything.   Listening to all alike it does not distinguish
between sycophants and others; but those especially seem to
make credible statements who excite this suspicion rather
than those who are eager to dispel it.

5.   From then on the wife is compelled to fear and
tremble no less before those living with her, those runaway
slaves and their wives.   She is forced to assume their position instead of the status becoming her, which has been
conceded to them.   When will she be able to live without
tears?   During what night?   What day?   What holiday?   When
will she not moan, lament and wail?   There are the constant
threats, gross insults, abuse—whether from a husband hurt
without reason or from coarse servants—surveillance and
spying.   All is full of trembling fear.   For not only are
her comings and goings the objects of curiosity, even her
words and glances and sighs are carefully scrutinized.   She
must be more quiet than a stone and endure everything in
silence, confined to her apartment no better than a prisoner.   Or if she desires to speak and to sigh and to go out,
she must supply a reason for everything, and give an account to those corrupt judges, I mean the servants and

group of domestics.

6.   If you like, intersperse among these heartaches
untold wealth, a costly table, a flock of servants, and
distinction of a noble family, great power, a wide reputation, celebrated ancestors.   In short, omit nothing that
seems to make this life enviable.   But after scrupulously
ennumerating all such advantages, compare them with this
pain and you will see no pleasure emanating from them;
rather the pleasure has been extinguished as surely as a
small spark is falling into the vast sea.   This is the result when the husband is jealous.   If this emotion ever
comes over the wife—and usually it does—he will be less
affected than his wife, the greater part of the mental anguish once again falling upon that poor creature.   She will
be unable to use the same weapons against the suspect.   For
what man will tolerate a wife requesting him to remain at
home all the time?

7.   Who among the domestics will dare spy on his
master and not immediately be thrown into the pit?   So she
will not be able to console herself with these devices, or
in fact vent her anger through words.   Once or twice her
husband will perhaps endure her ill-temper but if she persists in her incessant accusations, he will swiftly teach
her that it is better to bear such behavior in silence and
let her anger die down.   This is the case with jealous suspicion.   When the awful suspicion happens to be true, no
one will rescue the woman from the hands of the outraged
husband.   With the law on his side, he leads her whom he
loved the most to the court and has her executed.   But the
man avoids punishment by the law, although there is punishment in heaven that is reserved for God's judgment.   Yet
this is not enough to comfort the poor wife, who must undergo a long and pitiful death from magic potions, from poi-
sons that the adulterous women prepare.   There are some

women who do not need to plot against their victims, since
these have anticipated their end and have been carried away
by the violence of their despair. So that even if all men
rush into marriage, women should not pursue it, for they
could not claim that the tyranny of desire is so predomi-
nant in them, and they reap the greater share of hardship
from it, as we have shown.

8. Well then, you ask if this is true of all marriages. This element is at least not absent from them all,
but it is completely absent from virginity. The married
woman, even if she does not fall into this unhappy state,
will be caught in the expectation of it. For it is not
possible for a woman about to live with a man not to fear-
fully calculate all the misfortunes associated with a
shared life. The virgin, on the other hand, has been freed
of marital troubles and suspicion of them as well. This is
not true of all marriages, nor do I assert this. But if it
is not, many other difficulties exist and even if you avoid
them, you will be unable to do so entirely. Marital problems are just like the thorns that stick to your clothes
when you climb across a hedge. When you turn to pick one
out, you are caught by several more. So too in the case of
marriage: if you escape one problem, you are pierced by another. If you avoid one trouble, you stumble upon another.
In a word, it is impossible to discover a marriage free
from all unpleasantness.

LIII

A Marriage Based On Money Is Not
Enviable; Rather It Is Harder To
Bear Than A Poor One

But, if you wish, dismiss for now the annoyances.
Let us examine and set out what appears to be enviable in
marriage and what many people, what everyone often prays to

obtain from it. What then is this? The man who is poor,
simple and of humble origins longs for a wife from among
the great and powerful and very rich. But we will find
that this envied situation engenders no fewer misfortunes
than that abominable one mentioned above. At any rate,
the race of womankind is contemptuous and weaker, and therefore is more easily tripped up by emotion. But when women
have many pretexts for contempt, nothing stops them. They
are like a flame catching hold of a piece of wood: they are
carried away by an unheard of arrogance. They overturn the
order of things, making everything topsy-turvy. For the
woman does not let her husband keep his place of dominance
but with an insane arrogance banishes him from that rank
and escorts him to the station that is properly hers, that
is to say one of subordination. She becomes the commander
and chief. What could be worse than this irregularity?
And I am silent about the reproaches, the insolence, the
unpleasantness, which are more intolerable than everything
else.

LIV
Even If You Could Subordinate
A Wealthy Wife To Your Will,
The Unpleasantness Is Greater

If you should say—and in fact, I have heard many
people say when the subject is discussed: "only let her be
rich and well-off, and it is no job for me to deflate and
humble her pride." If you say this, first of all, you do
not recognize that that is very difficult to do. Next,
even if you were successful, there is no small price to
pay: for when a wife has been subordinated to a husband
through constraint, fear and force, it will be more burdensome and distasteful than when she commands with complete
authority. Why is that? Because this force destroys all

love and pleasure. When there is neither love nor desire
but in their place fear and a compulsion, what value will
such a marriage have henceforth?

LV
It Is An Insufferable Evil To Marry
A Man Better Off Than Yourself

This is the case when the woman is well-off. If it
happens that she has nothing but the man is rich, she becomes a handmaid not a spouse. Slavery replaces freedom.
Losing completely the liberty to speak that befits her,
she will be no better off than those bought with silver.
If her husband wishes to behave licentiously, to drink ex-
cessively and take to her bed a retinue of courtesans, she
must endure it all. She must be content or depart his
household. This is not the only bitter development. Because her husband is this way she will be incapable of
freely ordering the domestics and handmaids. She lives
like a woman among strangers enjoying what is not hers.
Living with a master, not a husband, she is forced to do
and suffer everything. If, to take another case, someone
wishes to marry a person similarly situated, again the
equality is ruined by the rule of subordination, although
the size of her property persuades the woman she is equal
to her husband. What, then, should you do when such great
difficulties engulf marriage? If a very few marriages
that can be counted on one hand avoid this, do not cite
them, for our purpose is to define things according to
what happens generally, not rarely.

LVI
The Married Woman Has
Many Causes For Grief

1. In virginity it is difficult, no impossible,

for this to occur, but in marriage it is not difficult.
And if so many disagreeable circumstances, if so many misfortunes, are produced in what is apparently good, what
can be said about acknowledged causes for sorrow? For a
married woman fears not just one death though she die only
once; nor is she anxious for one soul though she have only
one. She trembles for her husband, her children, for her
children's wives and children. The more the root spreads
out into more shoots, the more its cares abound. For each
one, whether a financial loss or illness or any other misfortune occurs, for each one she must beat her breast and
lament no less than the stricken themselves. If they all
die before her, the sadness is intolerable. If some survive but others die untimely deaths, she cannot find complete consolation in this fact.

2. For the fear for the living that always unsettles
the soul is no less than the grief for the dead. Surpris-
ingly, it is more severe since time soothes one's grief for
the dead, but anxiety for the living must either exist constantly or end in death alone. If we are not strong enough
in our own misfortunes, what kind of life will we lead when
forced to mourn for the tragedies of others? Oftentimes
many women of illustrious families, who have been brought
up with much luxury, have been given in marriage to someone in a powerful position. Then, suddenly, before being
congratulated for this, danger like a tempest or blast of
wind strikes and they sink sharing in the fate of ship-
wrecks. Although they enjoyed a thousand blessings before
marriage, they have succumbed to the extreme unhappiness
of marriage. But this, you may reply, does not usually
happen to everyone or all the time. Yet it is not alien
to them all either—and I will say again, such unhappiness
befalls some people through actual experience. And for the
many who escape this experience, there is the anxiety

caused by the expectation of it. But every virgin is removed from this experience and expectation.

LVII
On The Pain Present
In Every Marriage

1. But, if you like, pass over these considerations.
Let us examine now what has been assigned by nature to marriage and what no one, willingly or not, can avoid in it.
What are these troubles? Labor pains, childbirth and children. Yet let us take up again our earlier discussion and
reflect as far as possible upon the events preceding marriage, for only those who have been through it know exact-
ly what it is like. Courting time is at hand. One anxious
thought after another, various in nature, comes to mind immediately: what husband will the girl get? Will he not be
low-born, dishonorable, arrogant, deceitful, boastful, rash,
jealous, penurious, stupid, wicked, hardhearted, effeminate?
Of course, all of this need not be true for every bride,
but it must be anxiously pondered by them all. Since it is
not yet clear who will be picked as her husband, since
there is still uncertainty, her trembling soul dreads
everything. There is nothing like this that she does not
imagine. If someone should object and say that if she ex-
pects the opposite, she can be happy, know this well: the
expectation of good does not comfort us as much as the
fear of pain causes us distress. After all, only when
good things are expected with confidence do they produce
pleasure, but if unhappiness is merely suspected, it immediately confounds and disturbs the soul.

2. Uncertainty about future masters does not permit
the souls of slaves to be at rest. This is true also for
young girls: during the betrothal period their souls re-
semble a ship driven by a storm. Each day the family

either accepts or rejects prospects. One suitor today surpasses in reputation yesterday's champion, but another will
replace him in turn. And it is possible that the expected
bridegroom at the very doors of matrimony is dismissed emp-
ty-handed, and the family hands the young girl over to an
unexpected suitor. Women are not alone in this plight; men
have painful worries too. Yet it is possible for them to
make inquiries, but for a woman continually shut indoors,
how could she find out about her suitor's habits and ap-
pearance? This is the case during the betrothal period.
When the wedding day arrives, the woman's anguish intensi-
fies. Her pleasure diminishes as her fear grows that from
that very evening any disagreeable trait will appear in her
and she will fall far below his expectation. It is bearable to be held in esteem at the beginning and later to be
despised. However, if she appears insipid from the start-
ing-line, so to speak, when in the future can she be the
object of his admiration?

3. And do not ask what if she happens to be beautiful. Not even then does she escape this worry. At all
events, many women radiantly beautiful in the prime of life
are incapable of captivating their husbands, who neglect
their wives and hand themselves over to much inferior women.
Once this concern is laid to rest, another follows on its
heels. I omit now the unpleasantness arising from the payment of the dowry: the father-in-law gives it up without
enthusiasm because he pays it out of his own pocket; the
bridegroom, although eager to receive it all, is compelled
to collect it discreetly; and because of it the wife
disgraced by the delay of its payment and blushes before
her husband above all for having an unfeeling debtor for a
father.

4. Yet, once that anxiety is eased, the fear of
childlessness straightway replaces it. In addition, there

is the conflicting worry of too many children. Since the
future is unknown, she is disturbed by both these fears
from the beginning. If she becomes pregnant immediately,
once again joy is mixed with fear—nothing that has to do
with marriage is without fear. She fears that she might
lose in a miscarriage what has been conceived and being
pregnant her own life will be endangered. If, on the
other hand, the pregnancy is protracted, the wife does not
speak freely, as if she were in charge of the hour of de-
livery. When the time of birth is at hand, labor pains
rend and tear the hard-pressed womb for an incredible time;
such pain is sufficient by itself to overshadow the good
aspects of marriage. Other cares along with these trouble
her. The poor miserable girl, although so tormented in
this way by pain, fears no less than it that a damaged and
crippled baby be born instead of one perfect and healthy,
that it be a girl and not a boy. This anguish no less than
childbirth in fact disturbs women at that moment; for they
are not only accountable in these matters but also in those
over which they have no control. In each instance they
dread their husbands equally. They neglect their own safety in so dangerous a time and are anxious that something
not desired by their husbands happen. When the child is
born and gives its first cry, concern for its safety and
upbringing succeeds in turn her earlier cares.

    5. Even if the child is naturally inclined and
adapted for virtue, again the parents fear that their off-
spring will suffer something terrible, that he will die
prematurely, or that he will change into something wicked;
for good children grow into mean and wicked men, as well
as wicked children do into honest men. And if one of
these dreadful possibilities arises, it is more intolerable and painful for a woman than if it had happened
initially. But if all the child's goodness remains secure,

at any rate the fear of a change always persists for the
parents, whose souls are shaken and whose pleasure is
greatly undermined by it. However, all married couples do
not have children. Do you acknowledge in its turn another
reason for despondency? So, whether they have children or
not, who are either good or bad, parents are afflicted by
diverse and distressing cares. Then how can we call marital life the most pleasant of all?

  6. But again, if a couple lives in harmony, their
fear is that death will burst in and end their pleasure.
Rather, there is no longer only this fear and the expectation of it; there is also the knowledge that they must inevitably, without a doubt, advance towards death. For no
one can cite one instance in which both spouses died on the
same day. Since this is not possible, the alternative is
the necessity of enduring an existence far harsher than
death, whether the time together be long or short. On the
one hand, the more time there is for a shared life, the
greater the opportunity for deeper grief because the long
period of intimacy makes the separation intolerable. On
the other hand, if their period of intimacy is short, before there is a taste of love with its fulfillment and
when passionate desire is still in full bloom, the couple
mourns over the loss of this more than over the separation,
since they have been robbed of it. For different reasons,
in both cases the spouses are afflicted by similar grief.

  7. What should we say of the separations that take
place in the meantime, the long absences abroad, the anguish accompanying them, the illnesses? What has this to
do with marriage, you ask? Many women are often sick for
this very reason; having been maltreated and provoked
first by anger, then by despair, they bring upon themselves
a high fever. And even if they experience nothing like
this when their husband is home, and enjoy instead his

continual kindness, because of his absence they are once
again victims of these woes. But let all this be passed
over and let us in no way accuse the institution of marriage. Yet we will be unable to extricate it from the
following charge. What sort of charge is it? That marriage does not allow someone of sound health to be better
off than a sick man but reduces him to the same state.

LVIII
Marriage Is Not At All A Grand
State Even If It Avoids All Troubles

1. Do you want us to set aside all of these troubles,
and assume the impossible in our discussion by conceding
that marriage embraces at one and the same time all that
is good: many fine children, wealth, a wife with discretion,
beauty and intelligence, that it embraces unanimity and a
long old age? Include both a distinguished family and
great power, and do not let this common unfortunate fear
disturb them: the fear of a change in their fortune. No,
let every cause for despair, every occasion for anxiety be
removed. Do not let any other reason, including untimely
death, disrupt the marriage; rather let the entire family
meet death in one day, or, what seems to be far happier,
let the children survive as heirs, and let them conduct
both parents to their grave after a long old age. What is
the object of this? What advantage will be gained from
this much pleasure when they depart this world? To leave
behind numerous children, to have enjoyed a beautiful wife
along with luxury and everything else that I have just now
related, and to press on into a lengthy old age, how will
that help us before that court in matters eternal and
true? Not at all. Are not these assumptions but a shadow
and a dream?

2. Since we will be unable to derive any benefit or

solace from these things in the ages without end that will
receive us in the other world, we must regard as equals
the man who enjoys such things and the one who does not.
For if someone has had only one pleasant dream in one night
in over a thousand years, we will not claim that he possesses anything more than someone not enjoying this vision.
And yet, I have not said all that I would like. For the
temporal world is as far removed from the other world as
dreams are from the truth, no even more; and the present
life is not like one night in a thousand years in comparison to the future, but even in this the difference is again
much greater. Such things, however, do not pertain to virginity, for it departs from this world amply provided for.
But let us review the reason from the beginning.

LIX
Virginity Is Easy

The virgin need not make inquiries about her bridegroom, nor fear any deception. For he is God not man, a
master not a fellow-slave. The difference between the
bridegrooms is vast; but observe too the conditions of
their marriage bonds. The wedding gifts of this bride are
not bondage, parcels of land and just so many talents of
gold, but the heavens and its advantages. In addition,
the married woman shudders at the thought of death, among
other reasons because it separates her from her companion.
The virgin, however, both yearns for death and is oppressed
by life, anxious as she is to see her groom face to face
and to enjoy that glory.

LX
Virginity Needs Nothing That
Is Not In Our Own Power

1. Living in a state of poverty could not, as with

marriage, be disadvantageous for the virgin. Instead it
makes her, if she willingly endures it, more desirable to
the bridegroom. Likewise, a humble birth, a lack of beauty, and other such traits, they too are not prejudicial to
her. Why mention this? Even if she is not free, even this
status does not spoil her betrothal. It is enough to display a beautiful soul and to attain the first rank. There
is no fear of jealousy there, or distressing envy of another woman who has been united with a more brilliant
spouse. No one is similar or equal to him; no one approaches him even a little. But in the case of marriage,
although a woman has a very wealthy and powerful husband,
nevertheless she could discover another woman having far
more.

   2. In an extraordinary way, the superiority of those
surpassing us diminishes our own pleasure in surpassing
people inferior to us, and the great luxury of money,
clothes, a rich table and other excesses is able to entice
and attract the soul. And how many women enjoy these lux-
uries? Most people live in poverty, misery and toil. If
some women have such advantages, they are very few and far
between, and they are in conflict with the will of God,
for no one is permitted to luxuriate in these things, as
we have pointed out earlier.

LXI
Wearing Gold Creates More
Fear Than Pleasure

   However, let us assume once again that this life of
luxury is permitted and that neither the prophet nor Paul
speak out against jewelry for women.[199] What advantage is
there in much golden jewelry? None whatsoever, except
envy, worry and extraordinary fear. For the owners are
troubled not only when it is stowed away in a box and when

night has fallen, but also when they wear it. During the
day they live with the same—no, actually, greater anxiety.
Indeed, in the baths and churches there are women standing
about who are capable of mischief. Oftentimes, besides
these thieves, women wearing golden ornaments when pushed
and squeezed by a crowd do not realize that some of their
jewelry has fallen off. So, in any case, many women lose
not only this but, in addition, far more valuable necklaces
made from high-priced gems when they are pulled off and
fall to the ground. But enough of this fear; let even this
anxiety be laid to rest.

LXII
Wearing Gold Mars Your Beauty
And Increases Your Ugliness

    1. —Another man has noticed me, you say, and has
been impressed. —But he admires the ornaments, not the
woman wearing them; she is often reproached because of them,
as if she were adorned by them contrary to her true worth.
If she is beautiful, they violate her natural beauty, for
many ornaments do not allow beauty to appear unadorned and
detract from the greater part of it. However, if a woman
is misshapen and ugly, it sets off her unattractiveness
even more. Ugliness, however extreme, if it appears entirely by itself, seems only what it is; but when the splendor
of gems or the beauty of any other material exposes it, its
unsightliness is greatly increased.

    2. Dark skin appears darker when the light hue of
the pearl is laid upon it, as if the pearl were glistening
in the gloom; and a facial defect is pointed up far more
disadvantageously by brightly colored dress because it does
not permit the shape of the face to compete by itself before spectators, but is compared with that artificial and
irresistible beauty, and so its defeat is greater. Gold

that has been interwoven through clothing and the extensive
embroidery that one does and all other ornaments are like a
noble, healthy and vigorous fighter who repulses a mangy,
shabby and famished opponent.   In the same way, these embellishments attract the spectators' gazes and detract from
the outward loveliness of their owner.   They render her
even more laughable while making themselves worthy of extravagant admiration.

LXIII
What Are The Ornaments, What
Is The Beauty Of Virginity?

1.   But the ornament of virginity is not like this.
It does not detract from the one wearing it because it is
not corporeal but wholly spiritual.   Therefore, if the virgin is unattractive, virginity immediately transforms her
ugliness by surrounding it with an irresistible beauty.   If
she is in the bloom of youth and radiant, virginity makes
her brighter still.   Gems and gold and costly garments and
lavish, embroidered flowers of various colors and anything
else perishable in nature in no way adorn souls.   But the
following do: fasts, holy vigils, gentleness, reasonable-
ness, poverty, courage, humility, patience—in a word, disdain for everything in this life.[200]

2.   For the eye of the virgin is so beautiful and
comely that it has as a lover not men but the incorporeal
powers and their master.   It is so pure and clear it can
contemplate incorporeal instead of physical beauty, so
gentle and calm that it stands aloof.   It is not angered
by unfair people who continually cause annoyance; it even
considers such persons with kindness and graciousness.   So
great is the decorum surrounding the virgin that the intemperate, ashamed and blushing, check their frenzy when they
attentively look at her.   As a handmaid waiting on a

discreet mistress must follow her example, even if she
does not wish to, so the body of a soul so practiced in
virtue must harmonize its own impulses with the movement
of that soul. For her glance, her language, her demeanor,
her walk, in short, everything is defined by the discipline
within. It is like a costly perfume: although enclosed in
a vial, it penetrates the air with its own sweet smell and
suffuses with pleasure those inside and nearby, and even
all those outside.

3. So the fragrance of the virginal soul flowing
round the senses gives proof of the excellence stored within. The virgin, applying the golden reins of good behavior to everything, keeps each of the horses in perfect
rhythm. She forbids her tongue to utter anything discor-
dant or unsuitable, her glance to stray impudently or sus-
piciously, her ears to hear any improper song. She cares
too that her feet not walk in a provocative or pampered
fashion. She has an unaffected and artless gait. She
cuts away the decoration from her clothes and continually
exhorts her countenance not to dissolve into laughter, not
to even smile quietly, but always to exhibit a serious and
austere visage, one prepared always for tears, never for
laughter.

LXIV

What Is Experienced For Christ's Sake
Is Pleasurable, Even If Painful

When you hear the word tears, do not suspect anything sad; those tears are as pleasurable as the laughter
of this world. If you do not believe me, listen to Luke,
who says: "The apostles, although whipped, left the council full of joy;"[201] and yet this is not the natural effect of whips, which usually produce but a painful beating,
not pleasure and joy. But if the whips were not pleasur-

able, their faith in Christ was such that it prevailed over
the painfulness of the situation. If whips produced pleasure because of Christ, why are you amazed if tears also
produce the same effect because of him? This is why what
he called a close and narrow way, Christ calls a yoke useful and easily borne.[202] By nature, virginity is a burden
but, because of the resolution and the expectations of
those who successfully pursue it, it is extremely easy to
bear. Thus, you can see those who choose this life travel-
ing the close and narrow way more willingly than the wide
and spacious one, not because they will not be afflicted
but because they will be beyond afflictions and will not
suffer from them as others usually do. For this life does
have tribulations, but when we compare them to those of
marriage, they cannot be called by that name.

LXV
All The Hardships On Behalf Of Virginity
Do Not Compare With The Lonely   Pangs Of
Childbirth That Come With Marriage

Tell me, what does the virgin suffer during her whole
life that approaches what the married woman, who is torn
apart by birth-pains and loud wailing, endures almost every
year? The tyranny of this pain is so great that the holy
Scripture whenever it wants to intimate captivity, famine,
plague, and intolerable evils calls them all birthpains.
God has imposed this upon woman in place of punishment and
a curse—I do not mean birth itself but birth accompanied
in this way by labor and pain: "...in pain shall you bring
forth children," it says.[203] The virgin, on the other hand,
stands above this travail and curse, since he who has rescinded the curse of the Law has rescinded this curse too.

LXVI
It Is More Pleasant To Walk Than
To Be Carried About On Mules

1.   —Yet it is pleasant to be carried about the
marketplace on mules.   —This is merely an extravagant conceit devoid of all pleasure.   Just as darkness is not better than light, nor confinement better than freedom, nor
many needs better than none, so a woman who has not made
use of her own feet is not better off.   I pass over the
numerous unpleasant results arising from this that must be
endured.   For in fact, she cannot leave her house whenever
she wishes but must stay at home oftentimes, although some
business is pressing.   She resembles beggars who have had
their feet cut off and have no means of conveyance.   If
her husband happens to keep the mules completely occupied,
there ensue petty arguments and lengthy silences; but if
she without foresight does the same thing, she is angry
with herself for disregarding her husband and lets her ill-
treatment of him constantly gnaw at her heart.   How much
better it would have been if she had used her own feet—
after all, God made them for us for this purpose—and suffered none of these dire consequences than in her desire
to give herself airs to inevitably suffer from a painful
misunderstanding.   These are not the only reasons that
keep women at home.   This happens when one or both mules
have sore feet.   Also when they go to pasture (and this
occurs each year for a few days), a woman must again remain at home as if tied down, and she cannot go out in
spite of urgent business.

2.   If your response is that such a woman has been
saved from numerous chance encounters since she is not
forced to be seen all ablush by each of her acquaintances,
you seem to me to be quite ignorant of both what keeps
womanly nature from shame and what covers it with it.   For

appearing in public or retiring from it does not cause
shame, but rashness does since it does not check the soul
within; discretion and modesty, however, produce no shame.
Therefore, many women who have been liberated from their
apartments walk through the crowded market and are not
censured. In fact, they are much admired for their modesty. Through their demeanor, their walk, the simplicity of
their dress, they emit a brilliant ray from their inner
decorum. In contrast, not a few of the women who lead a
sequestered life have surrounded themselves with an evil
reputation. After all, it is possible for a woman who
has been shut off from society, even more than those who
go out, to make a display of herself before those who
wish it with greater recklessness and impudence.

                          LXVII
                  It Is Annoying To Have
                    Many Servant Girls

    ——But perhaps it pleases me to have a number of
maids. ——Nothing could be worse than this pleasure,
which involves as many worries as there are servants; for
you are inevitably disturbed and upset by each one's illness or death. But possibly this is tolerable, and so is
what is more troublesome still, namely, the daily effort
required to correct their laziness, to root out their
villany, to put an end to their ingratitude, and to correct all their other bad behavior. What is a bigger cause
of trouble and one very likely to occur with numerous
servants is the presence of an attractive girl among the
group——and this is bound to happen with many servants
since the wealthy class is just as eager to have pretty
ones as it is for many of them. So, whenever a servant
girl happens to stand out, if she captures her master's
fancy and puts him under her spell or has no more influ-

ence over him beyond being admired, the distress felt by
the mistress of the house is the same: she has been surpassed, if not in love, at least in youthfulness and admiration. Therefore, when what appears to be splendid
and enviable in marriage is so very trying, what can we
say about its painful aspects?

LXVIII
About The Detachment
Inherent In Virginity

1. But the virgin suffers from none of this. Her
house has been delivered from confusion, and all crying
has been banished from her presence. As in a calm harbor,
silence rules all within and another form of detachment
more perfect than silence possesses her soul because it
pursues no human activity but continually communes with
God and gazes more intently at him. Who could describe
the depth of this pleasure? What expression could suggest
the joy of a soul so disposed? It does not exist. Those
who delight in the Lord alone know the magnitude of this
joy and how futile it is to compare it with anything else.

2. —But the sight of much money gives the eyes
much delight. —How much better it is to look at heaven
and to derive a far greater pleasure from that. Just as
gold is brighter than tin or iron, so heaven is brighter
and more sparkling than gold, silver and all other metals.
This contemplation is free from cares but the contemplation
of precious metals is accompanied by anxiety, which above
all wholly spoils our desires. You do not wish to see the
heaven? You may see money deposited at the market. "I
say this is an attempt to shame you,"[204] as St. Paul would
say, seeing that you fly to the love of money. Yet I do
not know what to say, for embarrassment checks me at this
point. I cannot understand why almost all mankind, when

it could easily and without strain find enjoyment, does
not believe this state is pleasurable but enjoys instead
fretting and distraction and anxiety.

3. Why are people not delighted in the same way by
money deposited in the marketplace and money stored at
home? That at least is more brilliant and allows the soul
freedom from worry. ——Because, you reply, that is not
mine but the other is. ——Your pleasure stems from greed
then and not from the nature of money, since if this were
so, one ought to take delight equally in the other money.
If you say it is because of its usefulness, glass is more
useful. The rich themselves say so. They make drinking
cups mostly from this material. If by chance they must
make them from silver because of their affectation, they
set glass within beforehand and cover the exterior with
silver, thereby demonstrating that glass is more suitable
and fit for drinking, although the silver satisfies their
affectations and vanity. But what does the expression
'mine and not mine' signify? When I examine it closely, I
discover mere words.

4. Many people even during their lifetime are incapable of keeping money from slipping away from their
control. Those who keep it until the end, at the time of
their death both voluntarily and involuntarily are deprived
of authority over it. This is true of silver and gold, and
also of bathing-places, parks and houses. The expression
'mine and not mine' you can see is merely that. For all
commonly make use of these things; but those who appear to
be the owners receive a larger share of the worry than
those who are not. One set merely enjoys these possessions,
whereas the other takes great pains with these things but
gets the same enjoyment that the others do who are not
burdened with such cares.

LXIX
Sumptuous Tables Are
Full Of Unpleasantness

1.   If you admire extreme luxury, such as numerous
bits of cut-up meat, an extravagant consumption of wine,
unnecessary trouble over dishes, the artistry of the
maitre d', baker and chef, the throng of parasites and
guests, understand this well: the rich are no better off
than their chefs.   While the chefs fear their masters, the
masters themselves dread that the invited guests will object to something that has been prepared for them at great
expense and effort.   In this respect they are on an equal
footing with their servants, but in another way the servants have the advantage over them, for the masters fear
both critics and the envious.   Jealousies frequently arise
from such feasts and they do not cease until they have put
the host in great danger.   ——But it is often pleasant to
eat one's fill.   ——Come now!

2.   In fact, when headaches, stomach distention,
gasping for breath, vertigo, dizziness, clouded vision,
and more serious symptoms occur as a result of a life of
luxury, what pleasure will we take from all of this?   If
only our bad behavior and its damaging effects were limited to temporary pains!   But incurable diseases start
from such feasts.   Gout, consumption, a diseased mind,
paralysis and convulsions attack the body until the final
breath.   What pleasure can be named that counterbalances
these ills?   What austerity would we not choose in order
to escape them?

LXX
A Simple Life Is More Beneficial
And Sweeter Than A Life Of Luxury

1.   Frugality is different.   It is far removed from

all these vexations. It is conducive to vigorous health,
which you will discover is better than luxury. First, because you are in good health and are untroubled by any of
those problems, each of which by itself is able to check
and confound every pleasure at its roots. Second, because
of the food itself. What do I mean? Appetite produces
pleasure. Neither a surfeit nor satiety has this effect,
but a dearth and scarcity do. While scarcity is not present at the feasts of the wealthy, it is ever present at
those of the poor. It drips honey upon their fare more
than any maitre d' or chef could. For the wealthy eat
without being hungry, and drink without being thirsty, and
sleep before the need overcomes them. In contrast, the
poor become hungry or thirsty or tired and then satisfy
their needs, which especially increases their pleasure.

    2. And tell me, why does Solomon say that the sleep
of the slave is sweet? "Sleep is sweet to the laboring
man, whether he eats little or much."[205] Is it because of
his soft bed? But see, the majority of slaves sleep upon
the pavement or beds of straw. Is it because of their
security? But they control not even a small fraction of
their time. Because of their leisure time? But they do
not relax although exhausted by work and hardship. Then
what in the world is it that makes their sleep pleasant?
Their hard work and need for sleep before partaking in it.
As for the rich, unless the night has overtaken them im-
mersed in drink, they must lie awake, toss and turn, and
be distraught although they lie upon soft beds.

LXXI
Luxury Is Harmful For The Soul

    It would be possible to demonstrate elsewhere the
disagreeable nature of luxury, its penalty and its impro-
priety, by cataloguing how many diseases it imparts to the

soul, diseases that are far more numerous and severe than
those of the body. Luxury renders the soul soft, cowardly,
rash, boastful, licentious, overbearing, undisciplined,
irascible, cruel, sordid, grasping, servile, and unservice-
able for almost everything useful and necessary. But self-
sufficiency brings about the very opposite result. But
now I hasten to address myself to another matter; and so,
having added this one thought, let us return again to the
words of the apostle. If what seems to be enviable is
full of so much woe, and imposes upon the body and soul
such a torrent of disease, what are we to think of painful
things? For example, fear of the magistrates, popular up-
risings, plots hatched by sycophants and the envious—
troubles that especially plague the rich. Inevitably,
women have a larger share of these troubles, since they do
not endure nobly such changes in fortune.

LXXII
In Addition To The Other Evils, Luxury
Makes Changes In Fortune Intolerable

Why do I mention women? Men, too, unfortunately are
prey to such things. The self-sufficient man has no fear
of change; but the man who wastes his time in a pampered
and dissipated life, if he has bad luck and is forced into
poverty, will perish before enduring this change because
of his inexperience and lack of training. This is why St.
Paul said: "Such people will have trials in this life, and
these I should like to spare you." Then he says: "The
time is short."[206]

LXXIII
The Present Time Is Not For Marriage

1. Perhaps you will ask what has this to do with
marriage? It is very relevant. If marriage has been con-

fined to the present life and in the future people neither
will marry nor be given in marriage,[207] if the present speeds
to its end and the resurrection stands at our door, it
is not the time for marriage and possessions but for poverty and every other kind of wisdom of use to us in the next
world. The young girl, so long as she remains at home
with her mother, is occupied with childish cares. She deposits her little chest in the household treasury with its
store; the key and all authority are in her possession.
She is as solicitous of those little trifles as guardians
of important households are of what is in their charge.
However, when she must be betrothed and marriage forces
her to leave her father's house, then she is removed from
that world of trifles and her lowly position. She is compelled to manage the household with its many possessions
and slaves, to tend to her husband and other responsibilities greater than these numerous chores. This we too must
do when we reach the maturity appropriate for men. We
should abandon earthly things, which in reality are childish playthings, and place before our minds heaven and the
splendor of life there and all of its glory.

    2. For we have been united with a groom who demands
such affection from us that we give up for him not only
the things on earth and these small worthless objects but
also our own lives when necessary. Therefore, since we
must depart for the other world, let us free ourselves
from insignificant cares. If we were going to exchange a
poor house for a kingdom, we would not care about tiling,
timber, utensils and other household needs. So, let us
not worry now about earthly things, for the time already
summons us to heaven, as St. Paul said in his letter to
the Romans: "...for our salvation is closer than when we
first accepted the faith. The night is far spent; the day
draws near."[208] And again: "The time is short. From now

on those with wives should live as though they had none."[209]

3. What good is marriage for those not likely to
gain from it, who are in the same plight as those without
wives? What good is money? possessions? anything in life,
if its usefulness is from now on untimely and inopportune?
For if those who are to be brought forward before our
court to render an account of their errors think not of
their wives, and food and drink, and have no other concern
except their defense when the appointed day is near, it is
much more incumbent upon us, who are to appear not before
a terrestrial but a heavenly tribune to render an account
of our words, deeds and thoughts, to give no thought to
anything, either present joy or pain, but to concern ourselves exclusively with that fearful day. "If anyone,"
Christ says, "comes to me without turning his back on his
father and mother, his wife and his children, his brothers
and sisters, indeed his very self, he cannot be my follow-
er. Anyone who does not take up his cross and follow me
cannot be my disciple."[210]

4. But do you leisurely sit by indulging in your
passion for a woman and laugh? Are you indolent and given
over to luxury? "The Lord is near."[211] Yet do you fret
about money? "The kingdom of heaven is at hand." But do
you look to your house, your life of ease and other pleasure? "...The world as we know it is passing away."[212]
Why then do you wear yourself out in the midst of worldly
things that do not last but are used up, and neglect what
is sure and lasting? There will no longer be marriage or
birth pains, sexual pleasure or intercourse, an abundance
of money or the management of possessions, food or clothing, agriculture or seamanship, crafts or construction,
cities or homes, but some other system and way of life.
All of these will cease to exist in a little while. For
this is the meaning of: "...the world as we know it is

passing away." Therefore, why do we exert ourselves in
this way as if we will remain here for all ages? Why are
we anxious about things that often we will be separated
from before evening? Why do we choose a life of hardship
when the Christ calls us to one free from strife? "I
should like you," he says, "to be free of all worries. The
unmarried man is busy with the Lord's affairs."[213]

LXXIV
Why God Asks Us To Be Concerned Although
He Wishes Us To Be Free From Care

1. —How is it you wish us to be free from care but
impose in turn another cause for concern upon us? —Because this is not a cause for concern, just as tribulation
for Christ's sake is not tribulation, not because the nature of things changes but because the resolution of those
enduring suffering with pleasure can triumph even over the
nature of things. For the man who is concerned over what
he enjoys briefly, and frequently not even that long, would
reasonably be said to worry; but the man who will receive
greater returns for his attention would be ranked justly,
with good reason I think, with those without cares. Moreover, so great is the difference between each type of care
that the one compared with the other is not even thought
to be a source of anxiety, being so much more unsubstantial
and easily satisfied. All of this we pointed out in
earlier remarks: "The unmarried man is busy with the Lord's
affairs...but the married man is busy with this world's
demands."[214] But one passes away, the other abides.

2. Is this not by itself sufficient to demonstrate
the value of virginity? For this concern is superior to
the other, just as there is a difference between God and
the world. —Why then do you consent to marriage, which
pins us down to these cares and diverts us from the

spiritual? ——This is why I have said, Paul says: "...
those with wives should live as though they had none,"[215]
that those already enchained beforehand or about to be
make the bond looser in some other way. Since it is not
possible to break the bond asunder once it has been thrown
round us, make it more bearable. For it is possible, if
we wish, to do away with all that is superfluous and not
to add to the cares produced by the nature of marriage more
serious ones caused by our own stupidity.

LXXV
How It Is Possible While Having
A Wife, Not To Have Her

1. If you wish to understand more clearly what in
the world "having but not having a wife" means, reflect
how men without wives, the "crucified,"[216] live. How do
they live? They are not compelled to purchase a pack of
servants, golden necklaces, large splendid houses, and so
and so much acreage of land. Indifferent to all this, they
care for one cloak only and food for themselves. It is
possible to practice this philosophy although married. You
see, the statement above, "do not deprive one another,"
concerns intercourse only. In this matter Paul commands
couples to follow one another's desire, and he allows no
one to be his own master. But beyond this, the other way
of life should be adhered to, which affects one's dress,
mode of life and everything else. Moreover, a spouse is
no longer answerable to the other but husbands may, even
if their wives are unwilling, do away with every luxury and
its multitude of cares. In the same way, it is unnecessary
that the wife against her will beautify and preen herself,
and worry over trifles. This is a reasonable division, for
the former desire is physical and therefore meets with much
sympathy; one is not entitled to deprive one's spouse

against his will. The desire for luxury, on the other
hand, and excessive catering to oneself and useless cares
do not have their origin in nature. No, they are the pro-
ducts of laziness and much insolence. So Paul has not
forced married couples to be subject to each other's whims
in these matters, as he did in the other case.

2. This is the meaning of "having a wife but not
having one": it is to not accept the superfluous cares that
stem from women's feigned indifference and voluptuousness
but to assume as many additional cares as one soul imposed
upon us reasonably does, one that prefers to live philosophically and simply. That this is his meaning is revealed by an additional remark: "Those who weep should live
as though they were not weeping, and those who rejoice in
possessions as though they were not rejoicing."[217] For
those who do not rejoice will not be preoccupied with their
possessions, and those who do not weep will be incapable
neither of enduring poverty nor of shunning frugality.
This is the meaning of having a wife and not having one,
of having made use of the world and not having abused it.

3. "The married man is busy with this world's demands."[218] Therefore, since there is anxiety both in this
world and in the next but here it is without purpose and
in vain or rather even painful—"But such people will have
trials in their flesh,"[219] he says—but in the next world
it is the source of ineffable good, why do we not prefer it
instead, not only because it gives so much in return but
also because it is even by nature easier to bear? What
does the unmarried woman worry about? Is it money, servants, stewards, property and other things? Is she in
charge of cooks, seamstresses and the rest of the staff?
Of course not! None of these enter her thoughts. She reflects on one thing alone: edifying her soul and decking
that holy temple not with wreaths or gold or pearls, not

with cosmetics or eyeliner, not using other disgraceful
and debased methods, but with sanctity in body and soul.

4. "The married woman," he says, "is concerned with
pleasing her husband."[220] Paul has very wisely not scrutinized these matters, nor has he said how much women suffer spiritually and physically in their desire to please
their husbands. Their bodies they abuse with cosmetics
and mistreat with other punishments; their souls they fill
with stinginess, flattery, hypocrisy, pettiness and
thoughts both unnecessary and futile. But Paul intimates
this with one remark; he leaves the examination of this
point up to the conscience of his audience. Having demonstrated in this way the preeminence of virginity and
having extolled it to heaven itself, he changes the subject back to his acquiescence to marriage, since he always
fears that someone will think of virginity as a precept.
Accordingly, not satisfied with earlier exhortations, but
having said: "I have not received any commandment from
the Lord,"[221] and "Neither does a virgin commit a sin if
she marries,"[222] he repeats here: "I have no desire to
place restrictions on you."[223]

LXXVI
Virginity Is Not A Restriction
But Unwillingness Is

1. Someone would naturally be quite confused at
this point. For earlier Paul called virginity a release
from bondage and said he advises it for our own good, so
that we are without tribulation and are free from care,
since he has consideration for us and in all these ways
demonstrates that virginity is easily borne. But now he
says: "I have no desire to place restrictions on you."
What does he mean? He has not called virginity a restriction, certainly not. The restriction lies in choosing

this good under compulsion and unwillingly.[224] And indeed,
this is so. All that you accept under compulsion and
against your will, even if it is easily borne, is more intolerable than anything else and chokes our soul more
brutally than a noose. So Paul has said: "I have no desire
to place restrictions on you," intimating all the good inherent in virginity that I have alluded to and pointed out.
Nevertheless, after all of this, I leave the choice to you.
I do not drag you against your will to the virtue. I advised this course not out of a desire to afflict you but so
that your proper waiting for the Lord not be interrupted by
temporal affairs.

     2. Observe, if you will, Paul's wisdom at this point
too, how he has introduced once again an exhortation along
with his earnest prayers and, in giving his permission, his
counsel. For the phrase: "I do not compel you but advise
you," and the additional one: "to promote decorum and devotion"[225] show the admirable nature of virginity and what
we gain from a way of life in accordance with God. For it
is not possible for a woman who has become entangled in
human cares and who has been dragged hither and yon to be
completely devoted once all her attention and leisure time
has been divided among many things, I mean her husband,
the management of the household and all else that marriage
usually entails.

LXXVII
The Woman Who Is Anxious About Temporal
Things Would Not Be A Virgin

   —What is his response when the virgin busys herself
with human affairs and cares greatly for them? Come now,
does he drag her out of the chorus of virgins? —It is not
enough to be unmarried to be a virgin. There must be spiritual chastity, and I mean by chastity not only the absence

of wicked and shameful desire, the absence of ornaments
and superfluous cares, but also being unsoiled by life's
cares. Without that, what good is there in physical purity? Virgins are like soldiers: nothing could be more disgraceful for a soldier than to throw aside his arms and
spend his time in taverns; and nothing could be more in-
decorous for a virgin than to be embroiled in earthly affairs. For truly, those five maidens held their torches
and practiced virginity but they enjoyed nothing in return.
They remained outside the closed doors and perished.[226]
Therefore, virginity is beautiful because it removes every
pretext for unnecessary care and affords complete leisure
for works of God. If this is not so, it is much inferior
to marriage, since it surrounds the soul with thorns and
suffocates the pure and heavenly seed.

LXXVIII
Why Paul Does Not Sternly Upbraid
The Man Who Thinks He Is Behaving
Dishonorably Toward His Own Virgin

1. "If anyone," the apostle says, "thinks he is behaving dishonorably toward his virgin because a critical
moment has come and it seems that something should be done,
let him do as he wishes. He commits no sin if there is a
marriage."[227] ——What do you mean, "let him do as he
wishes"? You do not correct this mistaken opinion but instead permit the marriage? Why have you not said: but if
he thinks he is behaving dishonorably toward his virgin,
he is a poor unfortunate to think so admirable a state is
ignominious? Why have you not advised him to put aside
this suspicion and guide his daughter away from marriage?
——Because, the apostle says, such souls belonged to the
very weak, who crawl along the earth. It was impossible
to uplift all at once to the argument on behalf of

virginity souls so disposed. For a man who has been so
excited by worldly things and so admiring of the present
life as to think, even after such an exhortation, that what
is worthy of heaven and close to the angelic state is deserving of disgrace, how would such a man tolerate advice
promoting this course? And then is it surprising if Paul
has done this in the case of something that has been permitted when he does the same thing in the case of what has
been forbidden and is contrary to law?

    2. For instance: dietary laws, the acceptance of
some foods while rejecting others, were a Jewish weakness.
Nevertheless, there were among the Romans those who shared
this weakness. Paul has not only vehemently denounced
them, but he does something more than this. He disregards
the wrong-doers and censures those who attempted to prevent them with the words: "But you, how can you sit in
judgment on your brother?"[228] Yet he did not do this when
he wrote the Colossians; rather, with great authority he
upbraids them and treats the matter philosophically: "No
one is free...to pass judgment on you in terms of what you
eat or drink...."[229] And again: "If with Christ you have
died to cosmic forces, why should you be bound by rules
that say, 'Do not handle! Do not taste! Do not touch!'
as though you were still living a life bounded by this
world? Such prescriptions deal with things that perish in
their uses."[230]

    3. Why ever does he do this? Because the Colossians
were strong but the Romans still required much accommoda-
tion. Paul was waiting for faith to be first of all fixed
in their hearts. He feared that he would prematurely and
too quickly pull up the weeds and along with them the
plants of sound instruction.[231] So he neither reproves
them sternly nor leaves them uncriticized but in his criticism of others he subtly reproaches certain of them

without their being aware of it. For the phrase: "His
master alone can judge whether he stands or falls,"[232]
seems to curb the censor; but in truth its bite touches
the soul of the one rebuked. This shows that the preference for such actions is not characteristic of men self-
assured with their feet on the ground, but of those still
tottering, who do not stand fast and so risk a fall.

4. Paul follows the same principle here because of
the extreme weakness of the man ashamed of virginity. He
does not openly inveigh against him, but by commending
the other man, who closely watches his virgin, he deals
him a blow. What does he say? "The man, however, who
stands firm in his resolve."[233] This has been said by way
of comparison with the man who is indifferently and easily
influenced, who has never known how to walk or stand
steadfastly with much courage. Then, after he has clearly
observed that his argument is sufficient to sting that
man's soul, notice how he obscures it again by introducing
a motive not at all blameworthy. After saying: "The man
who stands firm in his resolve," he adds: "without constraint and free to carry out his will." Yet it would
have been consistent to say: but he who stands firm and
does not deem the state shameful, but this was too offen-
sive. He has therefore substituted another statement to
encourage the listener and allows him to arrive at this
reason. For it is not as serious to oppose virginity out
of necessity as it is to from a sense of shame. Indeed,
the first is characteristic of a cowardly and miserable
soul, the second of a soul perverse and unschooled in
judging rightly the nature of things.

5. But it was not yet the appropriate time for
these words. It is not right, even when there is a constraint, to forbid a young girl from choosing a life of
virginity. We must nobly stand firm against all that

interrupts this beautiful impulse. Hear what the Christ
says: "Whoever loves father or mother...more than me is
not worthy of me."[234] When we pursue something that seems
good to God, let anyone hindering us be an enemy and foe,
whether it is our father, mother or anyone else. But Paul
is still coping with what is imperfect in his listeners.
He writes: "The man, however, who stands firm...without
constraint." He does not stop his discussion at this
point, although the expressions "without constraint" and
"free to carry out his will" are equivalent.

6. But by the length of his speech and his persis-
tence in giving his permission, he encourages the simple
and small mind. He even adds to these reasons another:
"He who has decided in his heart."[235] For it is not enough
to be responsible: only when a man makes a choice and
reaches a decision does he act well. Then, so that you
do not think there is no difference between the two states
because of his great concession to marriage, Paul estab-
lishes again the distinction, no doubt timidly, but nevertheless he does so with these words: "To sum up: the man
who marries his virgin acts fittingly; the one who does
not, will do better."[236] However, for the same reason
again, he has not indicated here how much better. If you
wish to learn what it is, hear the words of Christ: "...
they neither marry nor are given in marriage but live like
angels in heaven."[237] Do you see the distinction, to what
height virginity lifts up the race of man all at once when
it is truly virginity?

LXXIX
The Followers Of Elijah Differed
In No Way From The Angels, And
Virginity Was Responsible For This

1. Tell me, in what way did Elijah or Elisha or
John, those genuine lovers of virginity, differ from the

angels? Not at all, except in so far as they had been
bound to a mortal nature. But in every other respect, if
you scrutinize them closely, you will find them not at all
inferior. Even what appears to be a serious defect in
them is an important reason for praising them. For although they inhabited the earth and were subject to the
limitations of a mortal nature, they were able to arrive
at that virtue: Do you see how much strength, how much wisdom they had? It is clear from the following argument
that virginity prepared them: for if they had wives and
children, they would not have lived in the desert so
easily or despised houses and the other conveniences of
life. As it was, released from all these ties, they
passed their lives on earth as if they were in heaven.
They had no need of walls or a roof or a bed or a table
or the like. They had heaven for a ceiling, the ground
for a bed, the desert for a table.

    2. And the very thing that seems to others to be
the cause of hunger, the barrenness of the desert, was for
those holy men a place of plenty. They had no need for
vines or wine-vats or cornfields or harvests. Plentiful
and sweet drink was supplied them from streams, rivers and
pools of water. An angel laid out for one of them a won-
drous and fabulous table grander than men are accustomed
to. It says, "One loaf sustained him for forty days without food."[238] The grace of the Spirit often nourished another of them who performed miracles, and not only him but
others through him.[239] And John, who was more than a prophet — no one born of woman has been greater[240]—required
no human nourishment. Neither food nor wine nor olive
oil sustained his physical being, but grasshoppers and
wild honey did. Do you behold the angels upon earth? Do
you comprehend the power of virginity? It has prepared
in this way those enmeshed in flesh and blood, who walk

along the earth and are subject to the necessity of human
nature, to approach everything as if they were incorporeal,
as if they had already obtained heaven, and were partaking
in immortality.

LXXX
The Meaning Of "To Promote
Decorum And Devotion"

1. Everything was superfluous to them, not only
what truly is more than sufficient, such as luxury, riches,
power, reputation and all the other objects of our dreams,
but also what is ostensibly essential such as houses,
cities and crafts. This is the significance of the phrase
"to promote decorum and devotion,"[241] this the virtue of
virginity. For while it is admirable and worthy of many
crowns to prevail over raging lust and curb a frenzied
nature, it is truly admirable when such a way of life is
practiced in addition; but by itself virginity is weak and
insufficient to save those possessing it. Many women who
now observe virginity could testify to this. They are as
inferior to Elijah, Elisha and John as the earth is to
heaven.

2. If you take away "decorum and devotion," you cut
out the very heart of virginity. But when you possess it
along with perfect conduct, you have the roots and foundation for goodness. For just as rich and fertile soil
knows how to nourish a root, so does perfect conduct know
how to foster the fruits of virginity, or rather the crucified life[242] is both the root and the product of virginity.
Virginity has annointed for the admirable race those noble
men. Clipping away all their chains, it permits them to
fly to heaven with unimpeded and nimble feet, as if they
were winged creatures. For when there is neither waiting
on a wife nor the tending to children, poverty is quite

easily borne. Poverty brings us near to heaven. It releases us from fear, anxiety and dangers, as well as other
troubles.

LXXXI
How Great A Good Poverty Is

The man who possesses nothing as if he had everything disdains all. He is very outspoken with officials,
and rulers, and the sovereign. For by despising possessions and advancing methodically, he will scorn even death
with ease. Since he is above these things, he will speak
openly with everyone and tremble in fear before no one.
But the man who has devoted himself to money is a slave to
it and also to his reputation, honor, the present life, in
short, to all human concerns. Consequently, Paul has
called it the root of all evil.[243] But virginity is capable of withering this root and inspiring in us another
virtue, which produces all good things: freedom, confidence,
courage, a fiery zeal, an ardent love of heavenly things
and a contempt for all earthly things. This is the meaning
of "decorum and devotion."

LXXXII
In Reply To The Statement That Those
Who Live A Virgin Life Pray to Come
Into The Bosom Of Abraham

1. But what is the knowing response of most people?
——The patriarch Abraham had a wife, children, possessions,
flocks and herds; and yet, inspite of all that, John the
Baptist, John the Evangelist, who both happened to be virgins, and Paul and Peter, resplendent in their continence,
prayed to depart into the bosom of Abraham. ——Who told
you this, my fine friend? What prophet? What evangelist?
——Christ himself did. For when he saw that the centurion

had much faith, he said: "Many will come from the east and
the west and will find a place at the banquet in the kingdom of God with Abraham, Isaac and Jacob."[244]   Lazarus too
was seen then faring sumptuously with Abraham by a rich
man.[245] —What has this to do with Paul? with Peter? with
John? Paul and John were not Lazarus, nor were the many
from the east and the west in the group of apostles. This
argument is futile and in vain.

    2. If you wish to know in short the apostles' re-
wards, hear the words of him who will grant them: "...when
the Son of Man takes his seat upon a throne befitting his
glory, you who have followed me shall likewise take your
places on twelve thrones to judge the twelve tribes of
Israel."[246]   Nowhere is there mention of Abraham or his
child or grandchild or his bosom receiving them, but there
is a reference to a dignity far greater than that, for they
will sit in judgment of the patriarchs' descendants. The
difference is clear not only in this respect but also in
that what Abraham obtained, many others will too. "Many
will come from the east and the west and will find a place
at the banquet in the kingdom of God with Abraham, Isaac
and Jacob." But no one else will obtain those thrones unless he is of this holy group.

    3. Do you still speak of flocks and herds, marriage
and children? —You reply, what if many of those who
lived a virginal life, after much effort, pray to retire
there? —Yet I will state a more serious possibility: that
many who lived a virginal life will obtain neither that
bosom of Abraham nor a lesser reward but will go to hell
itself. The virgins barred from the bridal chamber make
this clear. —By this standard, then, is marriage equal to
virginity or inferior to it? For your example makes virginity inferior. For instance, if Abraham, who had been
married, now lives amid ease and luxury, and those who

lived as virgins are in hell, this suspicion is left in
your mind. ——But this is not so, not at all. Virginity is
not only not inferior, it is far superior to marriage.
How? Marriage did not make Abraham what he was, nor did
virginity ruin those poor women. Other virtues of the
soul proved the patriarch to be illustrious, and other
wickedness in their lives delivered those women to the
fire. Abraham, though married, was eager to achieve the
virtues of virginity, by which I mean decorum and devotion.

4. But those women, although they chose virginity,
succumbed to a sea of troubles and the turmoils of marriage.
You answer by asking what prevents a married person with
children, possessions and everything else from being "devoted." In the first place, there is no one today like
Abraham or even similar to him in a small way. More than
those practicing poverty, he spurned wealth and possessions
even with a wife, and he triumphed over pleasure more than
those observing virginity. For they burn with passion
each day but he had so extinguished this flame and had
been so free of any passionate inclination that he not
only abstained from having a concubine but also banned her
from his house to remove every reason for quarreling and
discord. It is not easy to find such behavior today.

LXXXIII
The Same Standard Of Virtue is Not
Set Forth For Us And The Ancients

1. Aside from these considerations, as I said in
the beginning and will repeat now, the same standard of
virtue is not demanded of us and the people of the past.
Today it is not possible to be perfect without selling
everything, without renouncing everything, not just possessions and a house, but even one's own life. In the past
there was not yet an example of such great moral strict-

ness. ——Well then, do we live more strictly now than the patriarch? ——We ought to, and we have accepted this precept but we do not live according to it, and so fall far short of the proper goal. For it is clear to all that the trials set forth for us are greater. This is why Scripture when it admires Noah does not simply offer words of praise for him but adds: "Noah, a good man and blameless in that age, was pleasing to God."[247] He was not simply "blameless," but blameless in his own generation. For there are many kinds of perfection that have been defined differently at different times, and with the advance of time, what was once perfect becomes imperfect later.

2. For example, living in accordance with the Law was perfect once: "...the man who carries them out will find life through them,"[248] but Christ came and demonstrated this perfection was imperfect. He says: "...unless your holiness surpasses that of the scribes and the Pharisees you shall not enter the kingdom of God."[249] At that time murder alone was thought to be reprehensible, but now both anger and verbal abuse alone could send us to hell. At that time only adultery was punished, but now just looking at a woman lustfully does not escape punishment. At that time only a false oath was thought to originate "from evil," but now even swearing is so considered. For it says: "Anything beyond that is from the evil one."[250] The people of the past had demanded of them nothing more than loving those who loved them; but now this grand and admirable act is so imperfect that even after accomplishing it, we have no more reward than the tax-collectors.[251]

LXXXIV
It Is Reasonable That The Same Wage For
Same Virtuous Actions Is Not In
Store For Us And The Men Of The Past

1. Why in the world is not the same wage for similar

actions not fixed for us and for the men of the past? Why
must we display more virtue if we are to obtain the same
rewards as they? Because the grace from the Spirit has
been poured forth plentifully today and great is the gift
from the advent of Christ. It has made men perfect instead of childish. It is like us with our children: we
demand of them much better conduct when they have reached
maturity. We no longer admire them in the same way when
they accomplish those feats that we approved them doing
in their youth since they are now grown up. We ask them
instead to display much greater excellence than that. So
too has God not demanded from human nature outstanding
virtuous conduct in the first age of man, inasmuch as it
was too childish. But when it heard the prophets and
apostles and had obtained grace from the Spirit, God increased the importance of the virtuous conduct expected
from it—naturally, for he also fixed greater compensations
and much more splendid prizes for us today. No longer are
the earth and the things of it in store for those reaching
this goal but heaven and blessings surpassing our comprehension.

2.   Is it not strange therefore that men who have
come of age still persist in this small-minded way? In
the past, human nature had been divided against itself, a
victim of implacable war. Paul in his description of this
says: "...I see in my body's members another law at war
with the law of my mind; this makes me the prisoner of the
law of sin in my members."[252]   But now this is not the
case. "The law was powerless because of its weakening by
the flesh. Then God sent his son in the likeness of sin-
ful flesh as a sin offering, thereby condemning sin in the
flesh."[253]   Thankful for this, Paul has said: "What a
wretched man I am! Who can free me from this body under
the power of death? All praise to God, through Jesus

Christ Our Lord!"[254]

3. This is why we are punished fairly because although we have been released, we do not desire to run as
quickly as men who have been bound hand and foot; or rather,
even if we could run as fast, we have not thus been freed
from punishment. For those who enjoy a profound peace
ought to raise trophies far grander and more splendid than
those who are severely oppressed by war. If we intend to
be ever busy with possessions, luxury, wives and business
details, when will we be men? When will we live by the
Spirit? When will we give earnest consideration to the
things of the Lord? When we depart from earth? But then
it is no longer the time for work or action but for crowns
and punishments. Then, if a virgin has not oil in her
lamps, she will not be able to get it from others but will
remain outside.[255] And if someone arrives clothed in dirty
garments, he will not be able to go out and change his robe
but will be led off to hell's fire.[256] Even if someone
calls upon Abraham himself, it will be of no use then.[257]
When the appointed day comes, and the tribune has been
raised, and the judge seated, when the river swept with
fire, and the review of our deeds begun, we are no longer
permitted henceforth to strip away our faults but voluntarily or involuntarily we are dragged to the penalty they
deserve. Not only will no one be able to intercede for us,
even if by chance someone with the confidence of highly esteemed men, if Noah or Job or Daniel,[258] even if he pleads on
behalf of his children and daughters it will be of no use.

4. But it is inevitable that sinners be punished
eternally, just as the virtuous be honored. Christ has
declared that there will be no end for either. There is
eternal life, he says, and there is eternal punishment.
For when he welcomed those on his right and condemned
those on his left, he added: "These will go to eternal

punishment and the just to eternal life."[259]

 We must therefore make every effort here. The man
with a wife must be like him without one and the man who
is in fact without one must practice every other virtue
along with virginity, so that we do not in vain weep bit-
terly after our departure from this life.

AGAINST REMARRIAGE

1.   It is not surprising that inexperienced women
seek out relationships with men, the pains of childbirth,
and all the other things that marriage drags into the
homes of men; for as the proverb says, even so painful a
thing as war is sweet to the untried. But the fact that
women who have endured a thousand troubles and who have
often been persuaded by necessity to both call happy those
who have been freed from the cares of the world and curse
ten thousand times themselves, the marriage brokers and
the day on which the bridal chamber was prepared—that
these same women after so much despair desire again the
very same things, this above all astounds me and puts me
at a loss. I am compelled to look for a reason why women
pursue as desirable what they once, when they were involved in it, considered was something to avoid. Turning
over and over in my mind numerous considerations, with
difficulty I believe I have discovered at last the reason
for this; but there is no one reason or even only two but
rather several of them. For with the passage of time some
women forget the past and remember only the present. They
come to marriage as to a deliverance from the woes of
widowhood, but they discover in it other troubles more grie-
vious still and so make the same complaints again, just
as before. Other women who gape at the things of the
world and dote upon the glory of their present life, women
who in addition think that widowhood is disgraceful,
choose the hardships of marriage for the sake of empty
glory and because of excessive conceit. And there are
some widows who are subject to no one but their own incontinence. Although they try to hide their real reason
with the pretexts mentioned above, they return to their
former way of life.

I neither undertake to accuse and condemn these wom-
en because of this second marriage nor do I recommend such
action to another because it does not seem good to Saint
Paul, or rather to the Holy Spirit. For while he did say:
"A wife is bound [by law] to her husband as long as he
lives. If her husband dies she is free to marry [whomever
she desires], but on one condition, that it be in the
Lord,"[260] and while conceding to the widow the right to
remarry, he also said: "She will be happier, though, in my
opinion, if she stays unmarried."[261] So that no one sup-
pose that this injunction comes from man, he added: "I am
persuaded that in this I have the Spirit of God," indi-
cating that he wrote these words for the Spirit.

So then, let no one think that I say what I now will
say to reproach or to accuse those who are married. Truly,
it would be the ultimate folly and even the height of madness to cruelly condemn these women whom that saint did
not punish but spared, and to do this when we have a thousand faults ourselves. For if we are ordered to not judge
lest we be judged according to the same standard[262] and
not to judge severely those who err in other ways, but
rather to be indulgent and kind, you deprive yourself of
every allowance for your own behavior if giving your attention to a case you condemn others. Because of this
judgment against your neighbor, you make the judge disposed to be harsher with you. Thus, neither to accuse
nor attack these women do I come now to this topic; for
that which can exist "in the Lord" has been freed from
every accusation. "But on one condition," he says, "that
it be in the Lord." But just as when we speak on behalf
of virginity, in exalting it we do not dishonor marriage,
so when we speak about widowhood, while we do not consider
the second marriage to be among forbidden activities, we
do exhort widows to be content with their first husbands.

Yet, even though we agree that the second marriage is in
accordance with law, the first marriage is much better
than the second. Let no one think that the preeminence of
the one can be construed in a way that is detrimental to
the other. For we do not make this comparison with the
intention of relegating remarriage to an inferior rank.
Nevertheless, while we admit that remarriage is lawful and
left to our own discretion, we prefer and even esteem the
state that is better by far than this. Why is that? because it is not the same thing for a woman be the wife of
one man and the same woman be the wife of two men. For
she who was satisfied with the first husband has demonstrated that she would not have chosen him in the beginning if she had known well the experience of marriage; but
she who led a second bridegroom into the bed of the first
attests in no small way to her great love of the world and
attachment to earthly things. The former was not attracted
to another while her husband was living; but the latter, if
she did not commit adultery while he lived, at any rate admired many others besides him.

2. But to avoid making assumptions about her past
life, let us consider the matter itself. For just as virginity is better than marriage, so the first marriage is
better than the second. The widow is at the start inferior
to the virgin alone, but in the end she equals and joins
her; but the second marriage differs from virginity at both
points. Apart from this, the woman who bears widowhood
easily often exercises self-control even while her husband
lives; but she who endures the state grievously is ready
to live not with two or three men only but with several,
and can scarcely keep from sex when she is old. Therefore,
just as the one marriage is indicative of much dignity and
self-control, so a second marriage I would say is indicative not of licentiousness (I should hope not) but rather

of a soul weak and carnal, one tied to the earth and incapable of ever displaying anything great and lofty.

But if someone should say that the good is the same
whether it occurs once, twice or even many times—for,
the argument goes, it will be good in the same way, and
one would be praised more justly who makes use of it frequently; so that if marriage too is a good thing, he who
has practiced it continually is more admirable and more
acceptable than he who does so rarely—we will reply that
this sophism could deceive simpler people, but it will be
easily detected by those desiring to turn their attention
to it. For marriage is not called marriage because of
coitus (since in this way even fornication would be marriage) but because the married woman is content with one
man, and in this way the free and discreet woman differs
from the harlot. If a woman should be content throughout
her life with one man, this would naturally be called marriage; but if she leads into her house many bridegrooms
instead of one, I do not dare to call her conduct fornication, but I would say that such a woman is much inferior
to the wife who has not known another man except her husband. For that wife heard the Lord say: "For this reason
a man shall leave his father and mother and cling to his
wife, and the two shall become as one."[263] One woman
continued to cling to her husband as if he truly were her
own flesh. She did not forget the head was given to her
once for all time. The other woman did not consider
either the first or the second husband to be the same as
her own flesh; for her first husband was cast out by the
second, and the second by the first. She could neither
remember the first husband well since she devoted herself
to another after him, nor will she regard the second with
the proper tender love since her thoughts are divided between him and her departed husband. And so it comes about

that each one survives, and both are cut off from the respect and love due a husband from a wife.

What sort of emotion does she think her second
bridegroom feels when he is led into the bedroom of the
first and climbs up into his bed and sees his wife laughing and jesting at these developments? Violent emotion,
to say the least. Indeed he will not approach her with
much affection; for even if he is more insensible than all
men, he will not be so brutal that he feels no human emotion, even if she surrounds herself and her home with a
thousand ornaments. For already grief has fallen upon the
house and it does not allow undiluted joy to exist in it.
It is like what happens when a section of the walls of a
house is charred by fire and then lightly plastered: the
traces of soot mar the whiteness of the surface and are
unpleasant to the eye. So, in this case, even if the second husband thinks of many splendid things, in the midst
of them he becomes sad and the resulting mixture is without joy. For truly, even the slaves, the handmaids, the
gardeners, those who visit, the neighbors and the family
of the departed man are downcast at the turn of events
and sigh deeply. And if there are orphans? If very
young, they attach to their mother the deep hatred of
those who are capable of understanding the situation. If
they happen to be older, they communicate their aversion
more than everyone else. All of which, of course, the
laws take into consideration. They console those disturbed by these things, and in self-defense say that they
did not institute this second marriage for this purpose
or according to a principle but because they had feared
that something worse would occur. They have kept all
forms of gaiety from this marriage. No flute or clapping,
no wedding-songs or dancing, no bridal wreaths or the like
add to the festivities. Only after doing away with all

embellishments, do they lead the uncrowded husband to his
widow-wife, thereby all but proclaiming that everything
that the couple does is worthy of forgiveness but not approval, clapping and bridal wreaths.

    3. Why then, you ask, did Paul forbid young women
to remain as widows even if they were willing? For so he
writes: "Refuse to enroll the younger widows."[264] Paul
did not forbid those who desired to remain as widows,
rather they compelled him against his will to impose this
rule upon them. If you wish to learn the will of Paul,
hear what he says: "Given my preference, I should like you
to be as I am,"[265] that is, continent. Saint Paul would
not have been inconsistent or been caught in so great a
contradiction nor would he, who desired that all men be
continent, have forbidden women who wished to remain as
widows. What is the meaning then of "Refuse to enroll the
younger widows"? Come, answer me, why does he say this?
For what reason? He has not simply made a pronouncement,
he has even added the reason: "For when their passions
estrange them from Christ they will want to marry."[266] Do
you see that it is not those who wish to keep their widowhood, but rather, those who prefer to marry after being
widowed whom he forbids to remain as widows and to be appointed to that holy company? And he does so very wisely.
For if you should intend to engage in second marriages, he
says, do not profess widowhood; for breaking a promise is
much worse than not promising at all. He allowed therefore successive intimate relationships not as if he were
framing a law but as if he were making a concession. "I
say this," he says, "by way of a concession, not as a command because of your lack of self-control."[267] Thus, he
prescribes the second marriage because of another greater
evil and indicates that it is an excuse for the weakness
of many. But I assert that it is a weakness arising not

from one's nature but from one's deliberate choice.

Even as the virgin who is corrupted after the pro-
fession of virginity dared something worse than adultery,
so too the widow who professed widowhood once but then
trampled under foot her agreement with God will make the
same error and will be subject to the same punishment.
But—this will surprise you—the punishment will be swift
and much more severe. For it is not the same thing, as I
said in the beginning, for an inexperienced woman and for
an experienced woman to be caught in the same temptations.
Not only here does Paul make this point but he repeats it
elsewhere: "That is why I should like to see the younger
ones marry, have children, and keep house."[268] He adds
the reason why he desires this. What is it? "To give our
enemies no occasion to speak ill of us."[269] It is likely
that many widows at that time had lived more recklessly
and arrogantly after the death of their husbands, as if
freed from some constraining tyranny of their husbands
over them; and so they earned a bad reputation for themselves because of their audacity. Drawing them away from
this ruinous freedom, Paul leads them back to their former
yoke. He says that if a widow intends to secretly prostitute and dishonor herself, it is much better to marry and
"give our enemies no occasion to speak ill of us." Thus,
because he did not want to furnish opportunities for re-
buke or want the widow to live the wanton life of a harlot,
he prescribed second marriages. At any rate, listen to
how many accusations he makes against them. For the right
course is for them to have applied all their time to
prayers and supplications. "Besides, they learn to be
ladies of leisure," he says, "who go about from house to
house—becoming not only timewasters but gossips and busy-
bodies as well, talking about things they ought not."[270]
But Paul does not wish the widow to behave this way, but

rather that her attention be fixed continually upon spiritual things. "A widow who gives herself up to selfish indulgence, however, leads a life of living death."[271]

He desires the virgin also not to limit her goodness
to chastity of the body but to spend all her leisure time
in the service of God. "I am going into this with you,"
he says, "for your own good. I have no desire to place
restrictions on you, but I do want to promote what is good,
what will help you to devote yourselves entirely to the
Lord."[272] For he does not wish the virgin to divide her
attention but to be totally devoted to the spirit and the
things in heaven and to care for the things of the Lord.
He exhorts the widow too to conduct herself in this way.
He says: "The real widow, left destitute, is one who has
set her hope on God and continues day and night in supplications and prayer."[273] Whenever they spend their leisure
time, which should be spent in accordance with the gospel,
on what is not only superfluous and useless but even very
harmful to their whole life, Paul appropriately guides
them to remarriage. God gave the Jews the sabbath not so
that they simply do nothing but so that they abstain from
wicked activities. In the same way, both the widow and
the virgin choose this life not to simply avoid associating
with a man but to attend to the things of the Lord, to be
completely devoted to the service of God.

4. —Yes, you say, but it would be an insufferable
evil for a woman inexperienced in business to be compelled
to take up men's affairs. She will not be able to manage
for herself as her husband could and will gain only worries
and complete ruin. —Well then, have all women who have
not remarried lost everything they have? Are they deprived
of everything? Is it not possible to see a widow managing
her own affairs? These objections are pretexts and excuses
a dodge to hide their own weaknesses. For many women have

managed households much more ably than their husbands and
raised their orphaned children. Some women have added to
their possessions, others have not diminished them. For
even God at the beginning did not entrust everything to
men, nor did he allow the business of life to depend entirely upon them. A woman would be truly despicable if
she contributed nothing to our lives. Aware of this, God
portioned out to her not a lesser share, which he indicated at the beginning when he said: "Let us make for him
a helper."[274] To keep man from having presumptuous ideas
with respect to woman because he had been created first
and woman had been formed on his account, God used this
phrase and checked man's conceit. He thereby indicated
that the affairs of the world need woman no less than man.
What, then, are these matters and in which of them does
she join with us for the support of life? Since private
duties no less than public ones contribute to the present
order of life, in apportioning them God has entrusted to
men all that has to do with things outside the household
and to women things at home. If they alter this order,
all is ruinously undone. In this way each is much more
useful in his own sphere than the other.

    If, then, household matters depend upon womanly
skills and in this area a woman is much better suited than
a man (just as craftsmen are better in their crafts than
unskilled workers), why have we been so terribly alarmed?
For accruing and collecting wealth away from home is sole-
ly the duty of men. It is not right for women to make
profits; but protecting and keeping a close watch on ac-
cumulated wealth is her duty alone. Thus, if acquisition
seems to be more important than protecting one's goods,
nevertheless, without it acquisition is useless and superfluous. Yet often even when one does save, one's profit
brings no benefit but causes complete ruin because it is

difficult for a man making a profit away from home to
procure it justly——for these men most of the time make
the unhappy circumstances of others their business——; and
what has been brought unjustly and by force into a woman's
power is detrimental to her skill and her management of
household affairs. So that if making a profit is in one
way better than preserving one's gain, in another way it
is shown to be inferior, as when it contributes nothing
to the increase of existing wealth but even destroys what
is held in reserve. Why, then, has the widow feared that
the household business, which *she* was in charge of when
her husband was alive, will run afoul when her husband is
dead?

——But, you reply, the widow will manage more easily
when no one resists her or acts peevishly because he fears
her husband. For the slaves, managers and stewards, all
cower before him; they obey compliantly and without pro-
test. When this fear disappears, however, they all insult
his widow, make mischief, act boldly and disrupt everything. If she comes forward to defend herself by tortur-
ing, flogging and tossing them into prison, she is condemned and insulted. Charges are made against her by many.
——But if she crushes under foot the marriage covenant, if
she forgets her love for her departed husband and the
evening on which he was first united with her, the clapping, the wedding song, the bridal torches, the first embraces, the food and hospitality that he always shared •
with her and the words a woman must enjoy hearing from a
man——if she throws away all of this suddenly as if it had
not happened, if she opens the doors of her house to another and draws him to her former husband's bed, which is
privy to all that went on before, if she does this, will
she have no detractors or accusers? Will people not hate
her and call her heartless and untrustworthy, and say she

breaks contracts? Will they not reproach her with other
such remarks?

    5. Do not think that because Saint Paul acquiesced
to remarriage that it is praiseworthy and has escaped the
censure of many. Although it is above chastisement and
punishment, it cannot share in commendation and songs of
praise. In addition, it is prone to vice and is lewd and
out of a woman's mind neither during fasting nor at any
other time. Although far from being punishable, assuredly
it is not close to praise. Such acquiescence itself is
nothing else but an indication of much weakness and neglect of the soul. If, then, you have feared that you
would gain the reputation of audaciousness because of your
sharp reproof to the domestics, you must fear instead
earning for yourself the reputation of lewdness, dissolute-
ness and faithlessness. Aside from this, it will be possible for the widow to better see to her responsibilities
and make her life secure—and to not be faulted but even
praised by everyone. In return for this she will attain
the good that proceeds from God. For if she wishes to de-
posit her money in heaven and bury it, so to speak, in
that inviolate place, not only will it not be diminished
but it will increase. Such is the nature of this seed.
But if she is too weak to defer to that law and does not
desire to transfer all her wealth at once, let her consider again that even if she takes a husband she will not be
assured of getting the kind who adds to her property. If
he is one to increase her wealth, let her reflect not only
upon this result, but also upon the fact that she will be
led to quarrel in many ways with both God and men. If
her new husband belongs to the ruling class with much
power, he will force her at times to do and suffer many
things against her judgment, and what she had feared in
the course of her widowhood she will now submit to out of

greater necessity. In addition, it is likely that she
will make a very rapid change in her way of life. By being a widow, even if she diminishes her goods somewhat,
she will still keep the remainder with much security. But
if she has been tied to a husband who is powerful and involved in civic affairs or who pursues some other concern,
often she will lose everything at once; for the misfortunes of husbands must be shared by the wives living with
them.

     But if nothing of the sort should come to pass, tell
me, what profit would there be in choosing bondage instead
of freedom? Of what advantage is much wealth when one
cannot use it for what one wants? Is it not much better
to have a few things with authority over them than to possess everything in the world under the condition that a
woman submit herself together with everything else to the
power of another? I pass over now the anxieties, the
spiteful behavior, the reproaches, the envy, the rash suspicions, the pains of childbirth and everything else. In
a conversation with the virgin, in all probability these
things will be discussed, inasmuch as she is inexperienced
and untaught in these matters; but such talk will annoy a
widow, for it is useless to try to teach her what she
learned more perfectly through experience. It is well to
add this point: that the virgin once married will be intimate with her husband with more confidence and freedom
than the woman who has been widowed. For even if the widow's husband loves her as a wife, he would not love her
as he would a virgin bride. It is clear to all that the
love for virgins is more frenzied and impetuous by far;
but a husband will not embrace and love a widow whole-
heartedly because she knew another man.

     For we all, as I said, by nature either from jeal-
ousy or vanity or for some other reason I do not know love

those things above all that we have authority over and enjoy with no one else, and over which we ourselves have
been established as the first and sole masters. One can
see this is true of clothes also; we are not disposed in
the same way toward what has been used by another and
what is new. This is true also of houses and belongings.
We do not like a house that is given to us by another as
much as the one that we ourselves built. As for belongings, if they are new and used for the first time by us,
we treat them with great care; but if secondhand, we are
not very attached to them and dislike them so much that we
frequently pack them away. If this is our experience with
houses, clothes and belongings, consider the case of a
wife, who is more prized by a husband than anything else:
with what violent emotion are we likely to be affected?
Even if we share the former items with those who desire
them, it is not right for us to share a wife. We will die
before we endure that. Thus, a man with complete willingness allows the virgin to approach him, as I said, since
she is untouched and his very own and has never belonged
to another; but he will not view with the same love and
good will the woman who has been united with another at
an earlier time.

      6. Do not cite cases that are rare and exceptional.
Tell me instead about what commonly happens in practice.
This is not the only reason why the virgin will have a
greater share of freedom of speech, there are many other
reasons. A husband would easily be able to reproach a
widow on the grounds that he was scorned by her and could
bring forward as a sure sign of her contempt her faithlessness toward her first husband. He could silence her about
the past and future events too that perhaps will not occur.
For the deceased husband having been slighted will persuade
the living husband to suspect that he is being scorned,

even if it is not true. Not only will her second husband
harass her continually by casting these suspicions upon
her, even the domestics and handmaids, if not openly, in
secret at any rate, will whisper about her and make a
dozen jests at her expense. And if young children survive
the dead man, how will the widow bring them up? How will
she care for them? What orphans will have a harder time
than those who live to see another possess all the property of their father: his domestics, his home, his fields,
and the head of it all, his wife? How will they be able
to love her as a mother? And how will she be able to love
them? She is compelled to blush before them with shame
and cannot impart to them all her motherly love because
her thoughts are divided between them and the children of
the other man.

        —What then, you will say, if she is a very young
woman, and has enjoyed the company of her husband for a
short time only? —But I have said this to young women,
not to those who have grown old, for I will not argue with
them if they have remarried. If the lapse of much time,
their age and everything else did not persuade them to refrain from a second marriage a word from us will not at
all convince them. Instead, my argument is directed entirely to the younger women. —What if, you insist, she
is a young wife and has lived with her first husband for
only a year and she then remarries? Why will you not prefer
her to the woman who has spent twenty or thirty years in
marriage? —It is not I but Saint Paul who says: "She
will be happier...if she stays unmarried."[275] Why is
this? Even if she did live with a man for a long period
of time, at least she lived with one and the same man
only, who was chosen for her from the beginning; but the
other woman gave herself to two men and did this in a
short period of time. —You will reply that she does so

against her will; for if her first husband were alive,
she would not welcome another after him, but since he has
died prematurely, she was compelled to be united with a
second husband. ——What sort of compulsion is this, may I
ask? For I perceive a greater compulsion than the one you
mention, one that can persuade her to be content with her
dead husband, namely, her experience with the bitter things
in the world. The woman who has lived with something for a
long time with complete satisfaction will cling again to
similar things if she will obtain the same satisfactions;
but the woman who has experienced something so grievous
from the beginning, what does she intend by choosing this
same course, what does she expect from this difficult
trial? If someone who wishes to take a business trip is
shipwrecked as soon as he leaves the port before he has
made a profit, he will not calmly undertake the rest of
the journey. Nor is a woman likely to be enamored of
worldly things if she was expecting many pleasures from
marriage but experienced instead much sorrow, unless she
happens to be completely intemperate; or rather, even if
she should be very disposed toward worldly things and be
far too partial to them, the unpleasantness of the beginning is able to quench her desire. After all, we are
especially accustomed to continue in a pursuit when we get
off to a good start but when from the beginning, from the
starting point, so to speak, we perceive hardships and unpleasantness, we quickly back down because our enthusiasm
has been dampened.

Therefore, women who experienced premature widowhood
are likely to refrain from a second marriage to avoid suffering these same hardships again. She who keeps her
widowhood will have security and will not be apprehensive
about enduring such sorrow again; but she who undertakes a
second marriage will be compelled to expect this fearful

outcome. In addition, although widowhood is widowhood, nevertheless not all women will receive the same compensations for it. Some will get more, others less. Some women when they take up the yoke of widowhood in their youth will enjoy both more honor and more gifts, but others who became widows as old women will not receive the same treatment. Why is this? Because the former, although there were obstacles, endured everything because of the fear of God, while the latter did not suffer any sweat or toil. And how could they when there was nothing threatening them with violence? Thus, just as she who marries a second time is inferior to the woman who marries once, so she who keeps her widowhood from the time of her youth will be able to surpass by far the woman who has lost her husband in her old age. Although both had one husband, nevertheless one by her chastity outdistanced the other by many laps. So then, look not only to the hardship but to the compensation too. In this light, many right actions appear unpleasant to us because we mull over continually the hardships and exertion they entail and do not comprehend the wages in store for us.

But we should not proceed in this fashion. Rather we should weigh both sides, the hard work and the returns. In this way virtuous acts appear easy, just as they truly are. The hero arrives at excellence by estimating not only the injuries, misfortunes and death, but also by considering the trophies, victories and all the other honors. The farmer, too, starts up his work with an eye not only to the ploughing and the drudgery of digging but also to the threshing-floor and the wine-vats. In this way let us lighten the duress of widowhood with happy expectations, and we can do it much better than the hero or farmer since oftentimes many things over which they have no control shatter their hopes, whereas there is no one to crush our

hopes, unless we ourselves wish it. Let us not wish it at
all. Regarding the widow as not removed from the virgin
(and there are cases in which the widow has even surpassed
her, as when the virgin has clung to worldly things; but
"the real widow," according to Paul, "left destitute, is
one who has set her hope on God and continues day and
night in supplications and prayer,"[276] and abstains from
temporal things), let us undertake this contest to obtain
the crowns that await us there.

I have not said this out of necessity nor, as I said,
have I advised this with a view to condemning those who do
not wish to remain as widows; but we exhort and appeal to
widows not to be so attached to the earth for so long a
time, and once they have been released to remain free, to
seek heaven, and to exhibit the way of life found there,
and since they have been married to Christ, to do everything in such a way as becomes women who possess such a
bridegroom.

FOOTNOTES

[1] The heretical virgins were those who practiced virginity outside of the Church. Chrysostom had in mind the heresy of Encratism, which held that marriage was an evil in itself. See Anatole Moulard, *Saint Jean Chrysostome, le défenseur du mariage et l'apôtre de la virginité* (Paris, 1923) for a discussion of these heretical movements.

[2] 2 Cor. 11:2. The translations of all quotations from Scripture are from the *NAB* unless otherwise noted.

[3] Cf. Matt. 5:22.

[4] Matt. 5:44 and Luke 6:27.

[5] Cf. Matt. 5:47.

[6] Cf. Matt. 5:46.

[7] Cf. Matt. 25:33.

[8] Cf. Matt. 25:15-22.

[9] Cf. 1 Cor. 9:26 and Phil. 2:16.

[10] Cf. Mark 4:48, which echoes Is. 66:44.

[11] Cf. Matt. 8:12; 22:13 and 25:30.

[12] Rom. 2:9.

[13] 1 Cor. 7:7.

[14] Matt. 26:41.

[15] Matt. 19:12.

[16] 1 Cor. 7:25.

[17] Cf. John 8:44.

[18] Matt. 25:41.

[19] Cf. 1 Cor. 5:10 and 6:9-10.

[20] 1 Tim. 4:1-3.

[21] Cf. 1 Cor. 7:35.

[22] Cf. Matt. 23:2.

[23]Cf. Plato, *Republic* 7.527e and 7.533d.

[24]Ps. 45:14. My translation.

[25]1 Cor. 9:25.

[26]2 Tim. 2:5.

[27]1 Cor. 7:34.

[28]Heb. 13:4.

[29]Heb. 13:4.

[30]Plato, *Timaeus* 29a and 29e.

[31]Mark 2:24. (*NAB*: "I know....").

[32]Acts 16:17.

[33]Cf. Matt. 22:30 and Luke 20:36.

[34]Matt. 22:30.

[35]1 Cor. 1:35.

[36]1 Cor. 7:10.

[37]1 Cor. 7:12. My translation.

[38]Cf. Gal. 2:20.

[39]John 16:12.

[40]Matt. 5:32.

[41]1 Cor. 7:12-13.

[42]1 Cor. 7:40.

[43]Wis. 9:14.

[44]1 Cor. 7:1.

[45]Matt. 19:10.

[46]Matt. 19:12. My translation.

[47]1 Cor. 7:1.

[48]Matt. 19:12.

[49] 1 Cor. 2:14.

[50] Cf. Hesiod, *Works and Days,* 197-200.

[51] 1 Cor. 7:33.

[52] Gen. 1:28.

[53] Gen. 15:2. My translation.

[54] Cf. Eph. 4:13.

[55] Matt. 19:12.

[56] Cf. Gen. 6:7.

[57] Cf. Gen. 6:12.

[58] 1 Cor. 7:2.

[59] 1 Cor. 7:5.

[60] Ps. 50(49):20. Cf. Matt. 5:22.

[61] Is. 5:20.

[62] Hab. 2:15.

[63] Amos 2:12.

[64] Matt. 18:6.

[65] Cf. Matt. 5:22.

[66] Cf. Num. 12:1.

[67] 2 Kgs. 2:23-24.

[68] Cf. 2 Kgs. 1:9.

[69] Cf. Wis. 5:4-6.

[70] 1 Tim. 5:24.

[71] 1 Cor. 11:30-32.

[72] Cf. 2 Pet. 2:22.

[73] Ps. 73(72):5. My translation.

[74] Cf. Matt. 8:12 and 25:41.

[75]Cf. Acts 8:20.

[76]Cf. Num. 16:1 and 16:31.

[77]Cf. Exod. 14:28.

[78]Cf. Matt. 5:22.

[79]Cf. Acts 5:1-11.

[80]Cf. Josh. 7.

[81]Cf. Num. 12:1-8.

[82]1 Cor. 7:1.

[83]Cf. 1 Cor. 3:17; 6:15 and 6:19.

[84]1 Cor. 7:2.

[85]Cf. Prov. 6:28.

[86]Ps. 127(126):1.

[87]Ps. 127(126):1.

[88]Eph. 6:12.

[89]Cf. 1 Cor. 15:54.

[90]1 Cor. 7:1.

[91]1 Cor. 7:2.

[92]1 Cor. 7:3.

[93]1 Cor. 7:4.

[94]Matt. 5:33.

[95]1 Cor. 7:5. The *NAB* does not include "fasting."

[96]1 Cor. 7:3-5.

[97]Heb. 13:4.

[98]Joel 2:16.

[99]Cf. Matt. 18:24.

[100]Matt. 19:10.

[101] 1 Cor. 7:2-5.

[102] Cf. Matt. 5:28 and 31.

[103] Prov. 6:27-28.

[104] 1 Cor. 7:32.

[105] 1 Cor. 7:5.

[106] 1 Cor. 7:5.

[107] 1 Cor. 7:6.

[108] 1 Cor. 7:25.

[109] 1 Cor. 7:7.

[110] 1 Cor. 7:7.

[111] 1 Cor. 15:9.

[112] Gal. 4:12.

[113] Reminiscent of Jer. 3:1.

[114] 1 Cor. 7:7.

[115] 1 Cor. 15:10.

[116] Rom. 12:6.

[117] Matt. 19:12.

[118] 1 Tim. 5:12

[119] Luke 10:20.

[120] Cf. Matt. 5:6.

[121] 2 Cor. 6:4-6.

[122] Cf. 1 Cor. 7:38.

[123] 1 Cor. 7:7 and 7:8.

[124] 1 Cor. 7:8.

[125] 1 Cor. 7:9.

[126] 1 Tim. 5:11-12.

[127]1 Cor. 7:8-9.

[128]Cor. 7:39. The phrase "whomever she wishes," does not appear in the *NAB*.

[129]1 Cor. 7:28.

[130]1 Tim. 5:9.

[131]1 Cor. 7:9.

[132]1 Cor. 7:9.

[133]1 Cor. 7:10-11.

[134]1 Cor. 7:5.

[135]1 Cor. 7:11.

[136]Cf. Matt. 19:9.

[137]Cf. Matt. 19:8.

[138]Deut. 24:1. My translation.

[139]Cf. Eph. 4:31.

[140]1 Cor. 7:11.

[141]Gen. 3:16.

[142]Cf. 1 Cor. 7:2; 7:5; 7:9.

[143]Matt. 19:10.

[144]1 Cor. 7:4. My translation.

[145]Cf. 1 Cor. 7:21.

[146]1 Cor. 7:23.

[147]1 Cor. 7:25.

[148]1 Cor. 7:12.

[149]Matt. 19:12.

[150]1 Cor. 7:7.

[151]1 Cor. 7:8.

[152]1 Cor. 7:25.

[153] 1 Cor. 7:25.

[154] Cf. 1 Tim. 2:7.

[155] 1 Cor. 7:25.

[156] 1 Cor. 7:26.

[157] 1 Cor. 9:2.

[158] 1 Cor. 7:26.

[159] 1 Cor. 7:8.

[160] Cf. Eccl. 1:2.

[161] Cf. Luke 14:26.

[162] Gen. 2:18. My translation.

[163] Sir. 25:23.

[164] 1 Tim. 2:14.

[165] Cf. Job 2:9.

[166] Cf. Judg. 16:6.

[167] Cf. Num. 25:3, 5.

[168] Cf. 1 Kgs. 21.

[169] Cf. 1 Kgs 11:1.

[170] Sir. 25:18.

[171] Gen. 2:18. My translation.

[172] Gen. 1:26.

[173] Gen. 1:26. My translation.

[174] 1 Cor. 7:16. The *NAB* reads: "...that you will not save...."

[175] 1 Tim. 6:8.

[176] Isa. 40:6.

[177] Cf. Acts 18:24.

[178] 1 Cor. 7:16.

[179] 1 Cor. 7:27.

[180] 1 Cor. 7:28.

[181] Eph. 6:12.

[182] Cf. Matt. 25:1.

[183] I Cor. 7:26.

[184] 1 Cor. 7:29.

[185] 1 Cor. 7:29.

[186] 1 Cor. 7:32.

[187] Rom. 12:20.

[188] Rom. 12:20.

[189] Cf. 1 Cor. 2:2.

[190] 1 Cor. 3:2-3.

[191] Matt. 19:12. My translation.

[192] Matt. 5:45. My translation.

[193] 1 Tim. 5:6. The *NAB* reads: "A widow who...."

[194] 1 Tim. 2:9-10.

[195] 1 Tim. 6:8-9.

[196] Amos 6:3. My translation.

[197] Sg. 8:6. My translation.

[198] Prov. 6:34-35.

[199] Cf. Isa. 3:16-26 and I Tim. 2:9.

[200] I Tim. 2:9

[201] Acts 5:41. My translation.

[202] Cf. Matt 7:14.

[203] Gen. 3:16.

[204] 1 Cor. 6:5.

205 Eccl. 5:11.

206 1 Cor. 7:28-29.

207 Cf. Matt. 22:30.

208 Rom. 13:11.

209 1 Cor. 7:29.

210 Luke 14:26-27.

211 Phil. 4:5.

212 1 Cor. 7:31.

213 1 Cor. 7:32.

214 1 Cor. 7:32-33.

215 1 Cor. 7:29.

216 "οἱ ἐσταυρω μένοι," i.e. the ascetics. Cf. Gal. 6:14.

217 1 Cor. 7:30. The phrase ἐν κτήσεσιν does not appear in the Pauline text.

218 1 Cor. 7:33.

219 1 Cor. 7:28. My translation.

220 1 Cor. 7:34.

221 1 Cor. 7:25.

222 1 Cor. 7:28.

223 1 Cor. 7:35.

224 Cf. 1 Cor. 7:37.

225 Cf. 1 Cor. 7:35.

226 Cf. Matt. 25:10.

227 1 Cor. 7:36.

228 Rom. 14:10.

229 Col. 2:16.

230 Col. 2:20-21.

[231] Matt. 13:29.

[232] Rom. 14:4.

[233] 1 Cor. 7:37.

[234] Matt. 10:37.

[235] 1 Cor. 7:37. My translation.

[236] 1 Cor. 7:38.

[237] Matt. 22:30.

[238] Cf. 1 Kgs. 19:5. The citation is not textual.

[239] Cf. 2 Kgs. 4:38.

[240] Cf. Matt. 11:11; 3:4 and Mark 1:6.

[241] 1 Cor. 7:35.

[242] Cf. Gal. 6:14.

[243] Cf. 1 Tim. 6:10.

[244] Matt. 8:11.

[245] Luke 16:23.

[246] Matt. 19:28.

[247] Gen. 6:9. The *NAB*, in place of "was pleasing to God,"
reads: "for he walked with God."

[248] Lev. 18:5.

[249] Matt. 5:20.

[250] Matt. 5:37.

[251] Cf. Matt 5:46.

[252] Rom. 7:23.

[253] Rom. 8:3.

[254] Rom. 7:24.

[255] Cf. Matt. 25:1-12.

[256] Cf. Matt. 22.

257Luke 16:24

258Ezek. 14:14, 20.

259Matt. 25:46.

2601 Cor. 7:39. Bracketed words do not appear in the *NAB*.

2611 Cor. 7:40.

262Cf. Rom. 2:1, Matt. 7:1-2 and Luke 6:37.

263Matt. 19:5.

2641 Tim. 5:11.

2651 Cor. 7:7.

2661 Tim. 5:11.

2671 Cor. 7:6.

2681 Tim. 5:14.

2691 Tim. 5:14.

2701 Tim. 5:13.

2711 Tim. 5:6.

2721 Cor. 7:35.

2731 Tim. 5:5.

274Gen. 2:18. My translation.

2751 Cor. 7:40.

2761 Tim. 5:5.